MY PARENTS ARE AGEING,
WHAT THE HECK DO I DO?

MY PARENTS ARE AGEING, WHAT THE HECK DO I DO?

Understanding Australia's aged-care system to support older loved ones at home

CORAL WILKINSON

'A must read for anyone who wants to support their ageing parents to live at home as long as possible. The saying "knowledge is power" rings true here. Coral's personal and professional experience shine through in this practical guide to getting the right care to support your ageing parent at home. She explains the complex aged-care system clearly, providing readers with the knowledge they need to maximise the support services available. This book will also help people avoid the many pitfalls that are inherent in the system, by empowering them with the right information. Whether you're at the beginning of your caring journey and just starting to consider services, or your parent is already receiving services in the home, this book is highly recommended.'

Michelle Chaperon, Founder Carers' Circle – caring for ageing parents
www.carerscircle.com.au

'Navigating the world of aged care could have been totally disastrous. Then we met Coral. Suddenly our lives changed when our dad had a fall, plunging our family into this new world which can be very daunting to someone dealing with the hospital system and the health of their suddenly older and frail parents. See Me Aged Care Navigators were understanding, caring, thoughtful and very knowledgeable about how and which avenues would work best for dad. Coral was just like a family member who guided and explained all the information important to making our journey less bumpy. Coral and her amazing team have all the tools and equipment to guide anyone through this aged-care world that sometimes may seem totally overwhelming. Thankyou for ensuring the best aged care for our dad'.

Marylou Catalano, Cairns

'With this book, Coral has created an invaluable guide for those requiring extra support as they get older. Packed full of helpful real-life examples, *My Parents are Ageing, What the Heck Do I Do?* provides comprehensive advice, written in plain English, about how best to navigate the complex aged-care system and make the most of the funding available.'

Dr Kailas Roberts. Psychogeriatrician, Dementia Expert and author of *Mind Your Brain: The Essential Australian Guide to Dementia*

'See Me Aged Care provided us with a personal, engaged and professionally conducted service:

- It is grounded in long experience and knowledge/expertise about the complex system of aged-care support.
- It helped us successfully navigate the aged-care maze of programs, applications and services that at first glance seemed to be a complex "jigsaw" full of jargon and titles that we found very stressful.
- At all times, Coral dealt with us sensitively, sharing her deep knowledge and experience about pathways that would suit our circumstances best.
- She was honest about what was possible/probable and the best outcomes we might expect. She kept us up to date with the process as it progressed.
- We always felt we could phone or email any questions we had.
- We are now moving forward to the next steps after being approved for a "My Aged Care Package".
- See Me Aged Care still offers us support for this period of follow up "in-home" assessment too.

This service was suggested to us by our son and we feel that it was a very wise investment in our future.'

Les and Lyn Carter, Sydney

'The majority of our ageing relatives are frightened at the thought of having to leave their home to be in aged care. This book is vital if you want to support your ageing relatives to have the freedom to live in the comfort of their home while having the support they need to age gracefully and peacefully. It's a must read for everyone.'

Bree James, Author, Speaker, Coach

'I wish I had met Coral years ago when I had to start navigating the aged-care system for mum. See Me is a service with genuine interest in helping older adults and their family/carers to understand and get the services they need – they have the personal and professional knowledge. I can't wait to have Coral's book in my hands, it will be *the* aged-care guide in Australia! I work in the sector and I know how hard it is to get expert, honest advice. I recommend See Me because it is a business with values.'

Erika Quintero, Perth

'I had the pleasure of meeting Coral last year when I approached her about my beautiful mum requiring help to stay in her home. I found Coral to be very professional, with a great depth of wisdom and knowledge about aged care. She was able to make a detailed assessment of mum's needs and secured a Restorative Package, and then within six months a Level 2 Package. I am extremely grateful for the care and commitment to our request, and would thoroughly recommend Coral and her team's expertise.'

Madonna Brodie, Brisbane

'See Me Aged Care Navigators is a very professional and caring service that is a must to help you navigate the complexities of finding the right aged-care options. Coral is experienced in assessing needs and then helping families find the right care options. If you are looking for an experienced, knowledgeable, caring and professional service to assist you to find the right care, I highly recommend See Me Aged Care Navigators.'

Rita Merienne, Sydney

'Coral Wilkinson from See Me Aged Care Navigators is a mover and a shaker. She is the person to go to when families have a loved one who requires an urgent ACAT assessment. Coral is extremely knowledgeable, organised and efficient when navigating the difficult and confusing minefield of the aged-care system. She is our guardian angel, and we will be eternally grateful for her advice and professionalism when providing clarity and help for our father. We would highly recommend See Me Aged Care Navigators to help families to make decisions for their loved ones.'

Maree Poke, Cairns

'Coral and her team at See Me have been nothing short of amazing with the support they have provided, not only to me and my family personally but our members (Cairns & Community Dementia Carers Support Group). We feel so comfortable calling when we have questions or concerns, and are confident in their responses. The wealth of knowledge the team has is astonishing, and knowing that a lot of it comes from personal experience puts us all at ease.

'I cannot fault this company or the beautiful people running it; they are doing much-needed work in our community and we are so grateful for all that they have done and continue to do.

'If ever you are unsure of where to start in the journey of aged care or have a question about absolutely anything to do with the daunting nature of ageing, I can assure you See Me will either provide you with the best and most relevant answer or point you in the direction to obtain exactly what you need.'

Cairns & Community Dementia Carers Support Group, Cairns

'Recently my husband and I had ACAT review assessments coming up. Normally I would feel confident to deal with these myself. However, during this past six months I have faced multiple medical emergencies and am now on chemo. I just did not feel equal to adequately preparing for the assessments and getting the best outcome.

'See Me Aged Care Navigators were highly recommended to me, and contacting Coral was the best move I have ever made. From the very first phone call See Me have been empathetic, patient, punctilious, and have left no stone unturned in their commitment to getting us the outcomes we so desperately need. Their commitment to the individual is amazing – they really care about people! They are totally committed to making sure that they have presented reports which will ensure your best outcome … the outcome that you need.

'See Me put all of their training and research into preparing detailed reports for my husband and me, and forwarded these to our ACAT Assessor prior to our assessments. The Assessor informed us at the outset of the assessments how impressed she was with See Me's reports, and said she had all the information she needed.

'After a brief conversation and checking of pertinent facts, the Assessor advised that we were being given the much-needed highest rating. How wonderful – we had been so very stressed and achieved the outcome we so needed!

'The entire experience of dealing with Coral and See Me has been a great pleasure, completely stress free, and we are so impressed with the wonderful service they offer.'

Vivien Sweeney, Townsville

'After trying unsuccessfully for nearly a year to get my in-laws to have an ACAT assessment done, Coral was recommended to me. We set up a video conference (as my in-laws are interstate) and we were able to sit down as a family in the comfort and security of our own homes, at a time that suited us, while Coral walked us through the entire ACAT assessment via the video link. Her knowledge of the aged-care system is second to none. She was so wonderful at reassuring my in-laws about the process and really smoothed the path for them in terms of what to expect, the questions that would be asked and what it would mean for them once they had submitted their referral. This negated the need for my in-laws to see a GP for the referral as we were able to submit it ourselves under Coral's guidance.

'Coral was then available for any other queries we had once the process had begun. Her replies and information were timely and very thoughtful. My in-laws have complete faith in Coral's knowledge (as do I) and are now happily on a package with a provider. Coral gave brilliant and insightful information about what to look for in a provider also. I believe this is incredibly important so as to give each person the best use of their funding and to help them to understand that they are empowered to make decisions based on what is ideal for them.

'The aged-care system is complex and confusing, but with an expert like Coral guiding us through it was a much easier process and there was no stress. Coral is knowledgeable, approachable and so dedicated to her clients. Thank you Coral – I will be singing your praises to everyone!'

Michelle Brown, Perth

'Our experience with Coral and her See Me Aged Care Navigators was nothing short of wonderful. The minefield of red tape and difficult paperwork was made that much easier with her knowledge and kind guidance.'

Glenice Cann, Brisbane

'See Me Aged Care Navigators is a very professional service. After being confused and stressed trying to navigate the "My Aged Care" and "DVA" websites, I found Coral's team both knowledgeable and compassionate. They sorted everything out for my mother. Our family greatly appreciates the fantastic support Coral provides to us all.'

Raymond Woodhouse, Cairns

My sincere thanks to the following people who jumped on board early and committed to purchasing the book prior to print. Including your names in my book is my way of acknowledging your support during this adventure.

Thank you for caring.

Aida Wilkinson	Kym Byrne
Jill Morris	Charmaine Rogato
Lee-Anne Eager	Vivien Sweeney
Josh Auld	Laurie Coyne
Karen Scull	David Rutherford
Jeff Brown	Erika Schuele
Gwendoline Ann Robb	Jo Kite
Roger Brown	Cathy McKinney
Imogen Auld	Michelle Chaperon
Alan Wilkinson	Janine Wells
Sonya Waugh	Raymond Woodhouse
Deborah Ford	Tiffany Mason
Cynthia Collyer	Martin Dumbrell
Sandra Wilkinson	Frank Grainer
Tracey Roberts	Alison McGrath
Erika Quintero	Janet Booij
Marian Hearn	Suzanne Reeves
David Dall'Alba	Jean Barry
Janine O'Brien	Helen Thomas
Natalie McDonald	Carolyn Cummings
Linda Kemmis	Skye Danuels
Tania Tsatralis	Christine Holden

Kate Atkins

Leticia Moran

Stephen Devenish

Glenene and Pat

Rachael Sellars

Tracey Simmons

Liz Hardie

Tracey Smith

Katie Whiffen

Fiona Ross

Madonna Brodie

Dijana Cukanovic

Marylou Catalano

Alison Grose

Kylie Marks

Micaela Marchant

Katie Packer

Paul McNamara

Joanne Mugridge

Jillian Alexander-Sachse

Robyn Taplin

Elise Bertram

Carmel Boutchard

Diane Dell

James Michael

Deb Gartner

Glenda Daly

Michelle Brown

Wendy Booij

Jenny Edwards

Rose Downey

Charles and Eleanor Oxnard

Jo Langtree

Liz Brown

This book is dedicated to everyone who is supporting older loved ones at home.

That you care, matters.

First published in 2022 by Coral Wilkinson

© Coral Wilkinson 2022
The moral rights of the author have been asserted

All rights reserved. Except as permitted under the *Australian Copyright Act 1968* (for example, a fair dealing for the purposes of study, research, criticism or review), no part of this book may be reproduced, stored in a retrieval system, communicated or transmitted in any form or by any means without prior written permission.

All inquiries should be made to the author.

A catalogue entry for this book is available from the National Library of Australia.

ISBN: 978-1-922764-26-3

Project management and text design by Publish Central
Cover design by Pipeline Design

Disclaimer: The material in this publication is of the nature of general comment only, and does not represent professional advice. It is not intended to provide specific guidance for particular circumstances and it should not be relied on as the basis for any decision to take action or not take action on any matter which it covers. Readers should obtain professional advice where appropriate, before making any such decision. To the maximum extent permitted by law, the author and publisher disclaim all responsibility and liability to any person, arising directly or indirectly from any person taking or not taking action based on the information in this publication.

CONTENTS

Foreword   1

Glossary   5

Introduction   13

PART I:
Getting started: understanding My Aged Care   19

1. How do I start the conversation with my loved one?   21
2. The access point to aged-care services and support   27
3. What to consider before contacting My Aged Care   35
4. Who is eligible for aged-care services?   43
5. How to make a referral to My Aged Care   49
6. Appointing a My Aged Care representative   57
7. What happens next?   65

PART II:
Receiving entry-level support   71

8. What is the Commonwealth Home Support
    Programme?   73
9. What is the Regional Assessment Service?   79
10. What services are available under CHSP?   85
11. Who receives CHSP funding and why it matters   95

PART III:

Receiving coordinated home support   **101**

12. What are Home Care Packages?   103

13. What is the Aged Care Assessment Team?   111

14. What is Short-Term Restorative Care?   119

15. What is the Transition Care Program?   127

PART IV:

What else do you need to know?   **135**

16. What happens after an assessment?   137

17. How do we choose a provider for a Home Care
     Package?   143

18. What's the difference between fully managed and
     self-managed?   151

19. What do we do if care needs increase?   159

PART V:

The 2023 aged-care reforms and what they mean for you   **167**

20. What to expect next   169

21. A new aged-care program   173

22. A single comprehensive assessment process   181

23. Care Finders to support navigation of the aged-care
     system   189

24. What are a provider's care responsibilities?   197

Conclusion   205

References   215

About the author   219

FOREWORD
BY MARCUS RILEY

The aged-care system in Australia is very difficult to navigate. More and more people will need to engage with this system to access necessary care, services and accommodation and indeed a greater number of these people will rely on support from their loved ones in finding the right options within the care system. How does one know what to do in these often stressful circumstances? How do we find the right information to best help our older family members? How do we ensure they are getting the best possible care and receiving all that they are entitled to?

The aged-care system is full of acronyms, confusing jargon, online platforms, convoluted administrative processes, financial assessments, personal assessments, clinical assessments, myriad options and a whole range of things that we are meant to understand before making decisions. Huge decisions such as, which people are going to be permitted in to my Mum's home to provide (very) personal care or where my Dad might live for the final years of his life. This is an unfair situation for any person and their family, but that is the reality hence we need answers, guidance, accurate information and a clear path to follow.

This book, *My Parents Are Ageing, What The Heck Do I Do?*, is not only a wonderful starting point for any one wanting such guidance it also serves as an invaluable resource to keep coming back to as you continue to engage with the aged-care system – either as a family member or a person using services. Coral Wilkinson has the vast professional expertise as well as knowledge gained through her personal experience to clearly and accurately break down the complex aged-care system so readers can actually understand what everything means. With such an understanding one can then plan and make decisions on what to do, identify the right options and feel empowered! At a time in our lives that is normally filled with worry, guilt and stress having clarity about what to do and how to do it is an absolute relief.

In the text that follows all elements of the aged-care system are extensively, yet simply, deconstructed. From the necessary assessment stages to the roles of different Government agencies, the various service types and the role of providers are all laid out for your easy consumption. Even the Royal Commission into aged-care quality and safety is evaluated giving further context about this important service industry.

This book is a reference point you can keep coming back to. It can be a starting point, a source of reassurance, even a tool to use when advocating on behalf of your loved one. The author has laid out clearly the pertinent information that we all need to know as well as providing more specific details that will resonate for people at different stages of their aged-care journey. Once you've read this book the first time, keep it on hand so you can refer back and continually arm yourself with knowledge that is so very beneficial to you and your family.

Marcus Riley is a Past Chairman and current Director of the Global Ageing Network and sits on the steering committee for GAROP (Global Alliance for the Rights of Older People) and the UN's Stakeholder Group on Ageing. He has a distinguished record of leadership roles with international, national and state-based organisations, has led various Government committees and in 2018 was awarded the Global Ageing Influencer award by Ageing Asia. He is a passionate advocate for positive ageing and for the interests of older people; accordingly he is the author of Booming: A Life-Changing Philosophy on Ageing Well.

GLOSSARY

Aged Care Assessment Service (ACAS): the Victorian version of the ACAT. The ACAS assesses and approves people under the Commonwealth's aged-care program, the same as the ACAT, but in Victoria they chose to refer to themselves as a service rather than a team.

Aged Care Assessment Team (ACAT): the team of clinicians who assess and approve for a broader range of programs to support people at home. ACATs also assess and approve people to move into residential aged-care facilities, otherwise known as nursing homes. ACATs assess and approve for the Home Care Package program, Short-Term Restorative Care program and the Transition Care Program. They are also able to approve for services under the Commonwealth Home Support Programme (CHSP).

assessments: The method of enquiring and determining a person's limitations with their day-to-day activities and establishing how much support is required to assist them at home. Assessments are completed by both Regional Assessment Service (RAS) assessors and the Aged Care Assessment Teams (ACATs, and also the ACAS), however the depth of assessment is very different between these two assessment workforces. Assessments are ideally done in a person's home but can also be completed over the phone.

Care Finders: A new workforce, proposed to be introduced in July 2023. Care Finders are a recommendation from the Final Report *Care, Dignity and Respect* of the Royal Commission into Aged Care Quality and Safety. Care Finders are regarded as personal advisors. The function of Care Finders is to assist older people seeking services and support with information about the aged-care system and case management services.

Care Management: A dedicated role recommended from the Final Report *Care, Dignity and Respect* of the Royal Commission into Aged Care Quality and Safety. Care Managers should be qualified and experienced to support an older person with developing and implementing a personalised care plan, monitoring and reviewing their situation to ensure services and support are offered in a timely manner and adjusting the care plan to reflect a person's changing needs.

Commonwealth Home Support Programme (CHSP): The entry-level program that is funded by the Commonwealth Government, aimed at providing entry-level services and support to enable older people who only need minimal support to manage in their own home. CHSP funding is allocated to a select group of providers, which differs from the model of Home Care Packages. This funding is proposed to be merged into the new Support at Home Program in July 2023.

coordinated home support: the type of support a person receives from a Home Care Package. This level of support is assessed and approved by the Aged Care Assessment Team.

Coordinated home support differs from entry-level support, which is fragmented. The coordination of the home support is the responsibility of the Home Care Package provider.

entry-level support: the type of support a person is approved for under the Commonwealth Home Support Programme. Entry-level support is delivered by any number of different providers, hence it is regarded as fragmented rather than coordinated. No one provider takes responsibility for coordinating services under this type of support. Entry-level support is assessed and approved by the Regional Assessment Service.

Flexible Care program: another funding stream under the aged-care program that provides short-term options aimed at a restorative or reablement approach. Short-Term Restorative Care and the Transition Care Programme are two of the programs funded under this model. The duration of these programs is only weeks, but they are excellent programs and should be considered for people who need intensive support to literally get them back on their feet. Both of these programs are assessed and approved for by the Aged Care Assessment Team.

fully managed providers: Home Care Packages must be managed by a provider so that reporting and compliance with service provision aligns with government expectation. Fully managed providers coordinate all services and support for older people receiving a Home Care Package. Fully managed providers typically have their own workforce of carers or support workers. They subcontract to any other services required, and they often have their preferred subcontractors. Fully managed providers charge a higher admin fee, typically around 30% of your package subsidy because they do all the work for you.

Home Care Package (HCP) program: approved for by the Aged Care Assessment Teams. This program offers four levels of support, known as packages. The packages have an allocation of subsidy or funding attached to them. The Home Care Package program provides for coordinated support which differs from support from the Commonwealth Home Support Programme where support is regarded as fragmented because any number of service providers may be involved with your care.

Home Care Packages: different levels of coordinated support assigned to people who are living at home. At present there are four levels of packages, level one being the lowest and reflecting basic needs, up to a level four package for people with higher or more complex needs. Home Care Packages are only approved by the Aged Care Assessment Team. Your approval from the assessor will enter the national queue until a package becomes available, then you'll be assigned your package. This process takes some months.

My Aged Care: the gateway to government-subsidised services and support. For people seeking in-home support or entry into an aged-care facility (nursing home), My Aged Care is the point of registration to access the support you or your older loved one needs. My Aged Care is a call centre and website. The people you speak to at My Aged Care are not assessors, though they will complete an initial screening to attempt to determine which assessment team your needs align with.

My Aged Care referral: how an older person is referred into the system for in-home support or entry into an aged-care facility. A referral can be made over the phone or on the website. The older person themselves can make their referral to My Aged Care, or someone else can do it on their behalf. Before a referral to My Aged Care occurs, it is important to be clear about all the support you or your older loved one needs, so the referral is then forwarded to the most appropriate assessment team. I encourage people to refer themselves or have a family member who knows them well make the referral to My Aged Care.

My Aged Care representative: a person who is nominated by the older person to speak on their behalf with the My Aged Care staff. Having someone else's support, being able to relay information to My Aged Care and receive any documentation enhances timely and effective communication. There are two types of representatives: regular and authorised. Anyone can be appointed as a regular representative. The authorised representative can only be a legally appointed substitute decision-maker, for example an enduring power of attorney.

national priority queue: regarded as the waitlist to be assigned your approved Home Care Package. When the Aged Care Assessment Team approves a person for a Home Care Package, the package isn't assigned at that point. A person's approval enters the 'queue' until a package becomes available, then it is assigned. The assignment of the package can take many months. If your older loved one's needs increase while they are waiting for their package to be assigned, it is possible to ask the Aged Care Assessment Team for a Support Plan Review, so your loved one could potentially move to the front of the queue quicker and be assigned the Home Care Package sooner.

referral codes: otherwise known as approval codes, these are the reference numbers generated by either the Regional Assessment Service or Aged Care Assessment Team that relate to approved services or support funded under the Commonwealth Home Support Programme. Each reference number relates to the specific type of service or support approved. Your loved one may receive just a couple of referral codes or many after an assessment, depending on what their needs are.

Regional Assessment Service (RAS, pronounced 'raz'): A workforce of non-clinicians who assess older people for entry-level services and support. Entry-level services and support are for people who only need basic support to assist them at home. RAS assessors are funded by the Commonwealth Government but subcontracted by other organisations on behalf of the government.

self-managed providers: Home Care Packages must be managed by a provider so that reporting and compliance with service provision aligns with government expectations. A self-managed provider differs from a fully managed provider because they charge less in administration fees but they do not coordinate the support – you or your loved one does this. Self-management offers greater choice and flexibility with support from the Home Care Package, but it is up to you or your loved one to source support workers, nurses and allied health clinicians and manage expenses within your allocated funding.

Short-Term Restorative Care (STRC) program: A short-term program with a restorative focus for people at home. STRC is offered over eight weeks, and the goal is to restore a person's function, enhance their mobility or provide equipment that will make things easier or more achievable in the home. STRC is a clinician-lead program, meaning the aim is to have nurses, physios, exercise physiologists, occupational therapists, psychologists, podiatrists or massage therapists address aspects of your loved one's wellbeing that could be improved to enhance their ability to remain independent.

subsidies: the funding the government allocates to offset in-home support for people. The words 'subsidy' and 'funding' are often used interchangeably. For example, the subsidy for a level 4 Home Care Package, being the dollar value attached to that level of Home Care Package, is also known as the funding for that package.

Support at Home Program: the name of the new program that will merge the Commonwealth Home Support Programme and the Home Care Package program, to be introduced within the reforms in July 2023. At the time of writing, there is a lot of research, stakeholder engagement and discussion occurring as to what this new program will look like. We know there won't be any Home Care Packages under this new program but the different levels and different options for in-home support are yet to be determined.

Transition Care Programme (TCP): a program of restorative care designed to support people returning home after a hospital admission. The goal of this program is to provide clinical-orientated support to people to help them recover from the hospital admission and regain their optimal function and independence after returning home. This program is of 12 weeks duration, though people may not need this amount of time to regain their function and may receive the program for a shorter duration. The Transition Care Programme is funded by the Federal Government and delivered by states and territories as the approved providers. The states and territories who deliver this program also need to contribute towards the subsidy the Federal Government is providing.

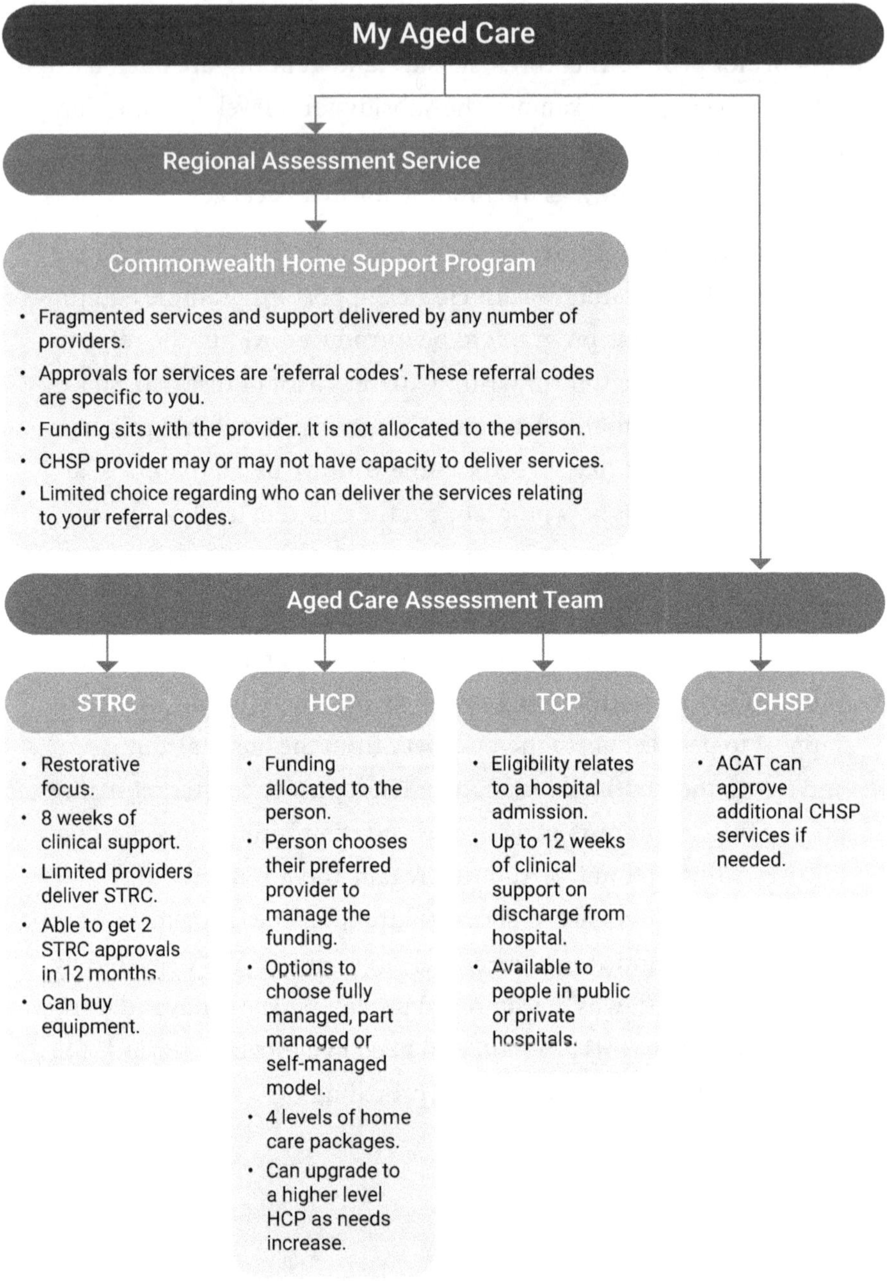

My Aged Care

Regional Assessment Service

Commonwealth Home Support Program

- Fragmented services and support delivered by any number of providers.
- Approvals for services are 'referral codes'. These referral codes are specific to you.
- Funding sits with the provider. It is not allocated to the person.
- CHSP provider may or may not have capacity to deliver services.
- Limited choice regarding who can deliver the services relating to your referral codes.

Aged Care Assessment Team

STRC

- Restorative focus.
- 8 weeks of clinical support.
- Limited providers deliver STRC.
- Able to get 2 STRC approvals in 12 months.
- Can buy equipment.

HCP

- Funding allocated to the person.
- Person chooses their preferred provider to manage the funding.
- Options to choose fully managed, part managed or self-managed model.
- 4 levels of home care packages.
- Can upgrade to a higher level HCP as needs increase.

TCP

- Eligibility relates to a hospital admission.
- Up to 12 weeks of clinical support on discharge from hospital.
- Available to people in public or private hospitals.

CHSP

- ACAT can approve additional CHSP services if needed.

INTRODUCTION

Australia's aged-care system is complex and confusing. The word that is repeatedly used to describe this system by the people using it is 'minefield'.

Sounds intimidating, doesn't it?

But it doesn't have to be.

This book has been written for older Australians who want to live in their own homes for as long as possible, and specifically to help their families and carers support them in doing so. This book will reduce the confusion, alleviate the stress and diffuse the overwhelm, by enabling you and your older loved one to engage with the system using the language and knowledge of an expert.

I've drawn upon my 18 years of extensive experience in older persons' care in the context of Australia's aged-care system to offer you an induction into how the system works and how to achieve the outcomes needed to support your older loved one in receiving the in-home services they need, now.

I'VE BEEN THERE

I understand what it's like to walk in your shoes. Being a daughter of ageing parents has given me personal experience as a carer.

My dad had dementia, Alzheimer's disease, and had four strokes in the last year of his life. I supported my family to care for my dad, at home, as he progressed through each stage of his dementia. Knowing what I do about the aged-care system allowed me to guide hospital clinicians about what options were achievable on discharge from hospital. It also allowed me to negotiate with his Home Care Package provider to adjust his care provision as his needs changed with his deteriorating health.

This knowledge placed our family in a position of empowerment and allowed us to access the most appropriate aged-care programs and source the most appropriate services and support to allow Dad to remain living in his own home, right through to his end of life.

I'm presently supporting my mum, who has just been upgraded from a Home Care Package level 2 to a level 4 package, meaning Mum was on a lower level of support but as her health deteriorated after emergency surgery and she became more dependent on my sister and me, she was upgraded to the highest level of Home Care Package. She lives by herself, has a few chronic health conditions, and she had emergency surgery last year which took some time to recover from. I manage her Home Care Package for her.

What I've been able to do for my older parents is what I want you to be able to achieve for yours. I want to enable ageing Australians and their loved ones with knowledge and know-how to make informed, planned and personalised decisions regarding their care at home, to optimise their independence and live their older years with confidence and control.

I know you want to support your ageing loved ones, but you're also raising your own family, invested in your own career and juggling the ever-increasing demands of day-to-day life.

How are you going to find the time to support your ageing parents?

Where do you start?

How do you start?

How does it all work?

What the heck do you do?

You'll find the answers in this book.

I WORK THERE

I'm Coral Wilkinson, your ally and expert navigator of Australia's aged-care system.

In 2019 I decided I couldn't sit back any longer and wait for the government or someone else to step up and provide clear information and guidance to people trying to support older loved ones in accessing the services they needed to continue living at home.

I took a leap of faith and launched my business, See Me Aged Care Navigators. I had been employed in the public health system as an assessor and delegate with the Aged Care Assessment Team for nine years and then as a Clinical Nurse Consultant (older persons) and Nurse Navigator (older persons).

I've participated in many state and federally funded projects orientated to better care for community-dwelling older people. I had the opportunity to provide subject matter expertise to SBS's *Insight* program, 'Caring for Ageing Parents', in 2021, discussing how older people can get better outcomes within the system.

I feel so passionately about the difficulties the system presents and the disadvantage it can cause to the people it is designed to assist that I made a submission to the Royal Commission into Aged Care Quality and Safety.

Aged Care Royal Commissioner Lynelle Briggs – in summarising her recommendations in the final report for the Royal Commission, titled *Care, Dignity and Respect* – stated: 'For too long the residential side of care has dominated the public conversation about aged care and determined the calls on the public purse. Our enquiry has confirmed over and over again that people do not want to live or die in institutions … Older people should be supported to remain in their own homes for as long as possible, because that is where they want to be.'

KNOWING WHERE TO START

My clients tell me they don't know where to look or how to begin to find support for their older loved ones. They describe the aged-care system as difficult and convoluted, and they're uncertain about the best way forward.

The confusion and frustration the system creates often causes people to disengage and seek information from local community support groups, neighbours and friends or social media. This second-hand information may not be accurate or appropriate to your individual circumstances. It is imperative that if you're thinking about your older loved one needing some assistance that you get the right information and adopt a proactive position to make that assistance happen.

It's important to understand who is best placed to begin engaging with My Aged Care (the gateway to Commonwealth-subsidised services and support for older Australians). My clients often think their GP is best to make the referral to My Aged Care, as the GP knows the person best, right? Wrong! *You* are best placed to make the referral to My Aged Care. You know your older loved one better than anybody else. The information you can provide to My Aged Care is key to receiving the right assessment and approval for the support that is right for your loved one.

People also trust hospital clinicians to make the referral to My Aged Care. While this option may be appropriate at a point of necessity, it doesn't provide you with information as to what happens next, how long you will be waiting for an assessment, what kind of assessment you'll receive and how to prepare for that assessment.

Understanding the context of the questions and the answers you need to provide for that referral or assessment is key to getting the best outcome for your ageing loved one. In this book, you'll learn how to answer the questions for a My Aged Care referral, you'll learn the difference between the two assessment teams, what services those teams can approve for and what the approval outcomes mean.

You'll learn how to get ahead in the queue for a Home Care Package if your loved one's health deteriorates and their care needs increase, or if your ability to provide ongoing care has reached its limit. And you'll be shown where to go for services and support outside the aged-care system.

This book will provide you with clarity, confidence and the ability to take greater control in supporting your older loved one at home.

Armed with an insider understanding of the system, you'll be empowered to talk with an ACAT assessor in their language, you'll be able to advise the My Aged Care call centre staff about the programs of support that reflect your loved one's needs at that time, and you'll be able to guide the RAS assessor to refer on to the ACAT because you'll know what's available within the different aged-care programs.

You'll also be able to enlighten your GP with a better understanding of the system, enabling a more coordinated approach to future care planning.

My promise to you, the readers of this book, is that after you've finished the final chapter, you'll feel confident to take control and assist your ageing parents, spouses, other family members or patients to get the support they need to remain living in their homes for as long as possible.

You'll achieve peace of mind and reassurance.

You'll know what action to take when your older loved one's health needs change.

And you'll feel confident knowing that the Home Care Package provider you've chosen is the right one for your loved one's needs. You'll go from being a passenger on a path that is fraught with hurdles and wrong turns to driving a clear pathway to the right care for your older loved one.

If you're seeking clear and accurate information to access the services and support your older loved one needs to remain living at home and you've become overwhelmed by the complexity of the system, this is the book for you. It will also be invaluable if you have a loved one who will be needing assistance soon. Or, if it's *you* who requires the assistance, you'll also get great value from these pages.

Written from my own experience and the experiences of thousands of families that I've supported through similar situations, this book will provide you with the knowledge and know-how to make this process easier, so that you know what the heck you have to do.

PART I

GETTING STARTED: UNDERSTANDING MY AGED CARE

CHAPTER 1

HOW DO I START THE CONVERSATION WITH MY LOVED ONE?

Knowing when and how to start exploring formal at-home services and support for your ageing loved one can be the most daunting step in the aged-care journey.

Perhaps you've noticed your ageing loved one is relying on you more and more to support them with their day-to-day needs.

You're cooking meals for them on the weekend and storing these meals in the freezer, to be reheated in the evening because they don't bother to cook anymore.

You're stopping by each weekend to tidy the yard and mow the lawn.

They're dependent on you for transport.

And they're calling you to ask about their appointments.

When my clients explain that they are providing this kind of assistance to their older loved ones and then ask me when the right time is to get some formal support into the home, I advise them the time is *now*. That this kind of support being provided by the family should be the trigger for a conversation about introducing formal support.

In this chapter, I'll discuss how to initiate a conversation with your older loved one about finding help for them at home.

WHEN AND HOW TO HAVE THE DISCUSSION

I've been in many family meetings with GPs or hospital clinicians where this scenario plays out: a discussion is occurring about getting some support into the older person's home. The older person is resistant and explains to the group that they don't need help because their adult children help them with their day-to-day needs, that they *like* to help them.

The older person is often unaware just how much support is being provided and the emotional and physical toll it's taking on their family members.

In these meetings, I've watched the adult children quietly sitting and saying nothing. I've seen the look of exhaustion on their faces. I've seen them looking at each other, gently shaking their heads, but no one is willing to raise the issue in front of their mum or dad.

Eventually one brave person will speak up, and will often be countered with, 'I'm not letting strangers into my home'.

End of discussion?

It shouldn't be. It's just not the right environment to be having this kind of conversation. Or the right time.

These conversations are to be nurtured over time and shouldn't be occurring as some kind of ultimatum or in response to a crisis. These discussions require compassion, patience and courage to initiate. And they need to be gentle and respectful conversations, taken in small steps.

If you're thinking about getting the family together for Sunday dinner or waiting until you see your loved ones at a special family gathering to broach the subject, this is not the best approach. You have good intentions of having everyone involved in the conversation, but if this is the first time the subject has been brought up or it has come off the back of a health event, this will be taken as an ambush by your older loved one. Your older parent is likely to become defensive (quite rightly so) and refuse to discuss the subject.

Instead, plan to have a few relaxed one-on-one discussions over coffee or tea, gently introducing the idea of simple formal support such as getting someone in to mow the lawn or accepting a cleaner. The lawn-mowing approach often works well in addressing the 'no strangers in my home' concern, as the lawn-mowing contractors will obviously stay outside.

And sorting a cleaner to do the more challenging domestic tasks such as cleaning the bathroom is a lot less confronting for an older person than someone cleaning their kitchen (which they may need too, but small steps are preferred).

Be honest with your loved one about the time it's taking you to provide all this support. Be calm and compassionate when you explain it's taking an emotional toll too. I've seen that light-bulb moment when a son or daughter tells mum or dad that they are struggling to divide their time between their own family and work commitments and providing the level of support that's required.

Acknowledging the benefits of introducing formal support leads into acceptance from your older loved one that you're developing a plan together that is beneficial to both or all of you. When your older loved one realises your Sunday afternoon visits would be more enjoyable chatting over a cup of tea or going for a drive rather than you cleaning the bathroom, they'll begin to see the value in getting support into the home.

A united approach is without a doubt a stronger position to place yourselves in as time goes on and frailty and dependence increase.

When the family is not on the same page

I was invited by both a GP and the family to a family meeting that was occurring at the GP's practice. The older lady at the centre of the discussion was living alone in her own home and her adult children, none of whom lived locally, were concerned about her wellbeing, specifically that she would have a fall.

The older lady was doing okay on her own. I had already been to her home twice previously to assess the situation and no alarm bells were ringing for me. She hadn't had any falls, she was managing to stay connected to her local community with transport via taxi, she had meals delivered and she managed her own appointments.

She wasn't receiving any formal support at all.

I thought the GP was asking me to the meeting to help him explain to the adult children what in-home support options were available for their mum. I didn't realise that the adult children had been having their own individual conversations with the GP about their concerns for mum, and though their concern was genuine, their solutions were different.

The older lady realised she had been ambushed, and not surprisingly became very upset. The children began shouting at each other, at mum and at the GP. The sons (one of whom was the enduring power of attorney) and the GP were trying to coerce mum into moving into an aged-care facility. The daughter was trying to explain to the sons and the GP that she would take mum into her home.

No one was listening to anybody else, and the older lady and I were sitting staring at each other wondering what was going on.

I gathered myself and took control of the meeting. I explained that mum was doing fine at present. The chorus chimed in and declared, 'she might have a fall!'

I replied, 'she will fall whether she is at home or in an aged-care facility'.

The chorus then declared, 'we don't live here, how do we know she is safe?'

I reassured the family that each time I went to visit mum, her security door was locked, I reminded them that each time they called her (daily) she answered the phone, and I also advised there were strategies we could put in place to provide them with peace of mind.

I suggested to the family that in the absence of mum receiving any formal support and doing okay by herself, moving her into an aged-care facility was a big step. I suggested we try getting support at home first and seeing how that went.

The mum agreed to this suggestion and eventually so did the family. And the GP went along with it too.

We manoeuvred the mum through My Aged Care and supported her with her assessment with the Aged Care Assessment Team. Within her level 3 Home Care Package, we were able to introduce support that allowed the older lady to remain living in her home for another 12 months.

* * *

Wondering how to start a conversation with an ageing loved one about accepting help beyond the family unit can be daunting. Our older loved ones have led accomplished lives. They've endured hardship. And they've prevailed. They're resilient and stoic and often too proud to acknowledge things at home are becoming harder to manage.

Accepting support from 'outsiders' just doesn't fit with the way our older loved ones were raised. Paving the way for introducing formal support starts with a compassionate conversation about your observations, the honesty to admit that your older loved one might need help beyond what you are able to sustain, and it requires the courage to face this change together.

Future planning founded in trust and understanding paves the way for better outcomes as you and your older loved one navigate each step in the aged-care journey.

THE ACCESS POINT TO AGED-CARE SERVICES AND SUPPORT

When people are doing their research and exploring what the options might be for support at home, they talk to people in their local community groups, they discuss options with neighbours and, if connected in the digital world, they seek answers in social media groups. Sometimes this topic may also come up in conversation with a GP, financial adviser or lawyer.

MY AGED CARE

It surprises me that there are many older people with family support who are unaware that there is a major Federal Government platform that serves as the access point to subsidised aged-care services and support, called My Aged Care. This is the point of contact for people who want to be assessed for those programs of support, which is in fact the majority of ageing Australians, whether they are pensioners or self-funded retirees.

My Aged Care is basically a call centre. It is also a website that provides an abundance of information relating to eligibility, assessments, and services and support. There is no cost to contact My Aged Care, or to progress through the assessment process for eligibility for services or support.

The staff at My Aged Care cannot provide you with personalised advice. They cannot comment on declining function, impaired cognition, chronic health conditions, acute medical situations or options for choosing a Home Care Package provider. My Aged Care is staffed by a non-clinician workforce who have received limited training about the different programs available to older people. Their responses to your questions are generic and scripted; they cannot provide you with advice about your specific circumstances. These staff also do not know what services and support are available in any local area, though the My Aged Care website lists service providers across the country. And eligibility for any of the programs when a person's needs change or when a person may be able to access more than one program at a time are things you won't get clear information on from the staff at My Aged Care.

Remember, it's a call centre designed to register and refer your loved one to an assessment service. My Aged Care are not the assessing team. They are not the people who provide the in-home care. They are a conduit to progress people through the system.

THE PROGRAMS AVAILABLE FOR OLDER PEOPLE

The Australian Government provides funding – known as 'subsidies' – to organisations for a variety of programs that provide support to people who want to remain living at home. (The government also subsidises accommodation in aged-care facilities, but for the purpose of this book residential care will not be explored.)

This funding for subsidised services and support is spread across many, many organisations such as local councils, state health services, and not-for-profit and private organisations, and these organisations deliver the relevant services.

Since July 2015, three levels of subsidised programs have been available to older Australians:

- the Commonwealth Home Support Programme (CHSP)
- the Home Care Package (HCP) program
- the Flexible Care program.

These subsidised services were available prior to this time, but they had different names.

These programs will be discussed in detail throughout the book, but let's have a brief look at each now.

The Commonwealth Home Support Programme

For older people wanting to remain living in their own home, the Commonwealth Home Support Programme (CHSP) is the entry-level program and supports older people who have minimal needs, the support being basic.

Support under CHSP is fragmented, and any number of different providers could be supplying services to the older person.

The Home Care Package program

This next level of support is for people with more complex needs. The Home Care Package (HCP) program provides for coordinated services and support. Once assigned a Home Care Package, this package – the funding or subsidy – belongs to the older person until they do not need it anymore. There are different levels of support with Home Care Packages, which are directly related to funding based on a person's need.

The Flexible Care Program

There is also the Flexible Care Program which focuses on re-abling people who are experiencing a functional decline, with the intent to restore function and potentially halt the need for a Home Care Package.

The flexible care programs are short-term, and there are different eligibility criteria compared to CHSP and HCP eligibility.

ACCESSING THE PROGRAMS

Regardless of what the older person's needs are, accessing these programs requires registration with My Aged Care.

Anyone can make contact with My Aged Care. The older person can make a referral, a family member or carer can make a referral on behalf of the older person, a GP can make a referral, and any nurse or allied health professional or even a Home Care Package provider can make a referral on behalf of the older person.

A referral can be made over the phone or via the website. The registration and screening process is similar for both phone contact and online referrals.

Whichever option you choose for registering with My Aged Care, ensure you have given thought to your older loved one and their situation. Good preparation for making that first contact – understanding how the conversation you have with the My Aged Care staff will influence the next step – is key to ensuring your situation is conveyed accurately and that you present your loved one's case to ensure access to the most appropriate program of support.

At that initial contact with My Aged Care, you will be asked a series of questions.

This process takes you through your registration and screening for services or support via My Aged Care.

Sometimes the My Aged Care staff will advise you that this registration process is also the screening process, sometimes they won't. Why you may or may not be advised that at initial contact screening begins is related to your understanding of the process and the experience of the staff at that time. At initial contact, the My Aged Care staff will take some details to register your loved one within the system. These details would be your loved one's name, date of birth, address and Medicare card number. This is to generate an individual registration number. When the registration is complete, it is your loved one's decision to proceed or not with screening. Being unaware that the next step is screening and preparation is key to which assessment team you'll be referred to, the screening process may not capture the extent of your loved one's situation if you are not well prepared.

Often people call My Aged Care to register for services and support after they've heard about the long wait times for assessments and receiving support. They're keen to 'get into the system' once they realise the long wait times.

During that initial call with My Aged Care, the staff may suggest they check if your loved one is eligible for support. It is at this point they are beginning to screen for the assessment team they'll refer your loved one on to.

Keen to 'get into the system', people want to know if they are eligible. It is more than probable that the person will be eligible, but your loved one being referred to the assessment team that is right for their needs requires preparation.

It's important to be well prepared to present a true account of what is going on at home for your loved one, so that from this point of registration you are channelled to the assessment team that is appropriate for your needs.

Then the My Aged Care staff will ask how your loved one manages activities of daily living. They'll ask if they need help with tasks such as cleaning the house, shopping and cooking. They'll ask if they have difficulty getting out of bed or a chair, or if they can walk easily. There is one brief question that touches on memory or cognition and mood.

The questions do not touch on continence or carer stress. Continence, carer stress and concerns with mood or cognition are significant factors to consider for the forthcoming assessments.

The answers you can provide to these questions will be 'yes', 'somewhat' and 'no'. There are no options to go into more detail. The disadvantage of not being able to provide more detail is that this brief screening process doesn't capture your situation fully or accurately.

In practical terms, what this means is that you'll possibly be channelled to the assessment team known as the Regional Assessment Service (RAS) rather than the Aged Care Assessment Team (ACAT), thereby limiting the choice of programs your loved one could be considered for.

The wrong assessment

My clients were a woman and her frail, elderly mother.

The elderly mother had moved into the home of her daughter and son-in-law. She was hearing and sight impaired and also cognitively impaired.

The daughter was providing significant support, assisting with personal care including showering and dressing her mum, attending toileting and continence issues, supervising safe mobility, preparing meals, supervising medication, coordinating doctors' appointments and providing transport.

The elderly lady had high care needs and a complex medical history. The daughter was exhausted and worried about how much longer she'd be able to sustain her caring role.

The daughter spoke with their doctor, who recognised the elderly lady's needs as being high and complex and actioned what she thought was a referral to the Aged Care Assessment Team via My Aged Care.

My Aged Care progressed the referral to an assessment team. An assessor phoned the elderly lady and assessed her over the phone. The daughter described this assessment to me as being a 'nice chat'.

The approvals the elderly lady received were under the Commonwealth Home Support Programme, not approval for a Home Care Package, which is what she needed.

The elderly lady hadn't been assessed by an assessor from the ACAT, she had been assessed by a Regional Assessment Service assessor.

The online referral that the doctor had completed did not include a detailed description of the elderly lady's needs, which resulted in the entry-level assessment being conducted and approval given only for entry-level services.

Understanding what had happened, I was able to contact My Aged Care again and provide the extra details required to demonstrate the high needs of this elderly lady and the risk of carer crisis with the daughter. The next assessment was appropriately undertaken by an ACAT assessor who approved the lady for a Home Care Package level 3.

In the next chapter we'll go into detail about how to make sure this does not happen to you.

* * *

Considering in-home services and support for an older loved one may lead you to conversations with older people who are already receiving some in-home support. It might see you discussing support for your older loved one with your GP or financial adviser, perhaps when you're seeking such professional advice for your own matters. And it may end up taking you into online support groups.

It's important to have these conversations and appraise the information objectively, but know that My Aged Care is where you'll need to begin to access the support you're trying to find for your loved one to allow them to remain at home.

CHAPTER 3
WHAT TO CONSIDER BEFORE CONTACTING MY AGED CARE

Hopefully you're beginning to understand how important it is to be prepared for your first contact with My Aged Care. Though the questions you will be asked at that first point of contact are basic and only provide for superficial answers, you still have the power to drive the conversation and convey the level of required support or dependence of your older loved one.

WHERE DOES YOUR LOVED ONE NEED HELP?

Before you make that first contact with My Aged Care, take some time to reflect on all the things your loved one needs help with, day to day. I advise my clients to write a list. I advise them to take a couple of days, at least, to write this list.

If the referral to My Aged Care will be for an older loved one you support at their home, the most accurate way of completing this list is to remove yourself from your caring role and ask yourself, 'Could they manage at home without my help?'

If you use this prompt to reflect on the amount of support required to keep your older loved one at home, you'll start to establish a very clear picture of their limitations.

Your list should include:

- How clean is the house? Are there unwashed dishes in the sink? Do you wash the dishes when you pop over for coffee? How clean is the bathroom and toilet? Is there dog hair accumulating on the floor? Is there dust accumulated on the tops of surfaces? Do the walls have mould?

  Your older loved one is struggling to maintain the cleanliness of their home and formal support is indicated.

- How are they managing to buy their groceries? Are you shopping for them on your way over to visit? Are the neighbours buying essential items for them? Have you arranged click-and-collect for them?

  If you answer yes to these questions, then formal support is indicated.

- How is their personal care? Have you noticed body odour? Are they wearing the same clothes every day? Is their hair brushed? Are they wearing their dentures?

  If you've noticed your older loved one's odour is a bit unpleasant, or you need to prompt them to have a shower or if you've noticed they are wearing the same clothes each time you visit then you'd be thinking that they are unable to shower without assistance.

  Not completing their personal care could be a sign of emerging cognitive decline or low mood.

What's The Situation?

Use this checklist as a guide to work out what your older loved one needs help with and how often

What do they need help with?	How much time does it take to support them?

Cleaning the house

Can they manage to keep the kitchen clean? Is the fridge clean? Is the bathroom and toilet cleaning neglected? Is dust accumulating on higher surfaces? Have the fans and air conditioners been cleaned?

Cleaning the house

Do you engage a private cleaner each week and then tidy up the bathroom on weekends? Add up the total time offered to support your older loved one with cleaning.

hours each week

Yard maintenance

Do you mow their lawn on weekends? Do the grandchildren mow the lawns? Do you pay for a lawn mowing contractor to mow their lawn? Who does the weeding or pruning?

Yard maintenance

Is someone else mowing the yard weekly or fortnightly? Who is doing the pruning, mulching and cleaning of the gutters?

hours each week

Grocery shopping

Do you take your older loved one to the shops and assist with shopping? Do you pick up groceries and drop them off on your way home from work? Do you arrange Click & Collect for them?

Grocery shopping

How much time does it take for you to drive to the shops, complete the shopping and drop it off to your older loved one's home and unpack?

hours each week

Preparing meals and eating

Do you cook meals on the weekends, freeze them and drop them over to your older loved one? Do you buy frozen meals for them? Have they lost weight recently? Has their preference for food changed?

Preparing meals

How much time does it take you to prepare meals for your older loved one? Do they have a special diet that requires additional time to prepare? Do you have to be there to ensure they eat?

hours each week

Mobility and transport

Do they use a walking stick or 4WW, do they lean against the furniture or walls to stabilise themselves, are their shoes comfortable and sturdy or have they had a fall? Do they have trouble getting out of a low chair or out of bed? Are they dependent on you for transport?

Mobility and transport

Will they only negotiate stairs when someone else is present? Can they only attend appointments if you take them, ensuring they don't fall getting out of the car? Should you consider a disability parking permit?

hours each week

Laundry

Can they only manage to handwash underwear and small items, can they remove the sheets from the bed, wash the sheets, hang them out and remake the bed?

Laundry

Do you wash the towels and sheets each weekend? Can they reach the clothesline? Do they hang the washing over the furniture to dry?

hours each week

You can use a checklist like this as a guide to work out what your older loved one needs help with and how often.

And if you need to stand with them and supervise them showering or help them get undressed or even wash their back, this situation reflects someone who cannot manage to shower independently.

- Do you check on your loved one's boxes of medicine when you visit, or do you fill their Dosette box for the week? Is there medication still in the Webster pack that should have been taken two days ago?

This situation means that your loved one needs help with medications.

Forgetting to take medication begins to form a more complete picture of what else they may be failing to remember, and could point towards an undiagnosed issue with cognition or mood.

- Has your loved one had a fall recently and is now struggling to get out of a chair or bed?

Maybe they haven't had a fall but you've noticed getting out of a chair or bed is becoming more challenging for them. Maybe they've decided to sleep in the recliner chair instead of their bed because it's too difficult to get out of bed.

This situation demonstrates assistance being required to complete this task.

There are many more considerations for you to add to that list. These include:

- Who mows the lawn, and how often?
- Who does the pruning, weeding or mulching?
- Are you cleaning their home for them on weekends? Or have you arranged a private cleaner for them?

- Do you do their weekly laundry and re-make the bed when you visit on weekends?
- Who changes light bulbs, arranges for the fans or air conditioner to be cleaned, or sources someone to water-blast mould from pavers or the driveway?
- Has your loved one lost weight?
- Is this weight loss related to reduced appetite, poor dentition, increasing difficulty swallowing, or have they lost interest in food?
- Are you cooking meals every weekend and freezing them, so your loved one can defrost them instead of cooking their own meals?
- Is there expired food in the fridge?
- Have they been experiencing tummy upsets? Have you noticed their milk gets left out on the bench when you come over to visit?
- Are they experiencing constipation or faecal incontinence? Have you noticed their underwear is soiled when you put a load of washing on for them?
- Have you noticed an odour of urine on your loved one? Are their bed sheets wet? Is there a towel covering the sheet or have they removed the sheets and put a towel on the mattress instead?
- Have you noticed wads of urine-soaked toilet paper or tissues concealed around the home?
- Have they needed to go to the GP more often to be diagnosed with a urinary tract infection?
- Do they have bruises or skin tears?
- Are they leaning on furniture or the walls to keep themselves upright when walking?

- Can they only walk with you at the shops if they have a shopping trolley to lean on?
- Do they need to sit and catch their breath after walking?
- Do you make their appointments for them, call them to remind them of an appointment the following day, and then pick them up and take them to the appointment?
- Have they disengaged from friends or community groups that they previously enjoyed?
- Do you find them still in bed when you go around to visit at 10am?
- Do they ask you the same questions or tell you the same stories over and over again?
- Are they beginning to tell you stories that just don't sound right?
- Are they misplacing objects and blaming it on someone stealing their possessions?
- Are they failing to pay bills on time? Have you already taken over this task for them?
- Is their behaviour changing from the kind of person they used to be?
- Have they forgotten where they parked their car at the shopping centre and called you to ask you where it is?
- Have they had an accident while driving?

This list is not exhaustive, but it should make you stop and think about how many simple day-to-day tasks you're providing support with.

Individually, these tasks don't seem like a lot, but putting it all together will give a true picture of the amount of support required to allow your loved one to remain living in their home.

Your list should have detailed answers to these questions. You should retrieve this list for any conversations you have with anyone who is aligned with aged-care services and be prepared to assert your situation.

* * *

The toll it takes on a child, spouse or other family member to provide this level of support often goes unacknowledged, until something else happens and the carer realises they have hit their limit, that they are so tired they don't have capacity to support their loved one during or through this recent event.

Carer burden, carer stress or carer crisis are big red flags for considering formal support in the home. Acknowledging your own fatigue and being able to articulate this during a My Aged Care screening or with any assessments thereafter is important for ensuring an assessor realises that the role you fill providing a high level of support is unsustainable.

CHAPTER 4
WHO IS ELIGIBLE FOR AGED-CARE SERVICES?

The easier question to answer here would be who *isn't* eligible for aged-care services because eligibility for such services in Australia is very inclusive.

Eligibility considers a person's age, being 65 years and older, or 50 years and older for First Nations people.

Eligibility for aged-care services in Australia also considers a person's functional and cognitive limitations (what they can and can't do for themselves), declining mobility or recent falls, or a change in carer status. A hospital admission can also make a person eligible for some aged-care programs.

ASSESSING LEVELS OF FUNCTIONING

The My Aged Care website has an eligibility checker, and the following questions are asked of a person seeking clarity about their eligibility.

- Are you over the age of 65?

- Which of these activities can't you do independently?
    - getting out of bed or chairs
    - walking
    - going to the toilet, wiping and re-dressing
    - taking a bath or shower
    - getting dressed
    - eating a meal
    - preparing a meal
    - taking medicine
    - basic housework
    - driving or taking public transport
    - shopping for groceries
    - managing money and paying bills.

Based on your loved one's responses to these functioning questions, you'll then be asked to respond to a few more questions about each task, noting *how much* of each task your loved one can or can't do.

If you've ticked 'Basic housework' as an area your older family member has trouble completing independently, the next section will seek to ascertain how much of the basic housework they can do.

For example, they can do all normal basic housework, only somewhat complete light housework or are unable to do any housework.

In elaborating on the tasks you have noted as not being able to be completed independently, there is no room or free text space to describe the situation in detail.

Completing this eligibility checker on the My Aged Care website will give you an instant answer about your loved one's eligibility.

Unless completely independent and needing no help whatsoever with any aspect of day-to-day living, it's likely your loved one will be eligible for some kind of aged-care program.

Thinking they are okay

My mum is 81 and relatively well and able for her age. She is stoic and just gets on with things, not making a fuss or asking for help.

My sister and I support Mum though, and while she recognises her day-to-day activities are easier with our support, she would not think to contact My Aged Care and refer herself, because she would just get on with it, managing as best she could.

The support my sister and I provide includes ordering Mum's groceries online and dropping them over to her, cooking meals (though she still cooks simple meals for herself too), and supporting her with doctors' appointments and accompanying her to those appointments to ensure she's understood everything the doctor has explained to her. We also clean her unit, purchase equipment and mobility aids that enhance safety within her home, and encourage her to attend group exercise classes.

You would be forgiven for thinking that my mum isn't eligible for or in need of aged-care services, but she is eligible and does receive services. Mum receives a Home Care Package and has done so for three years.

These tasks that my sister and I assist Mum with are on top of the support she receives from her Home Care Package.

Could Mum manage without our support? Probably not, at least not safely – there would be an ongoing risk with regard to mobility, nutrition, mood, cleanliness of the home and health literacy.

There are many, many older people living at home and struggling to manage their activities of daily living and thinking they are okay, that aged-care services are only for people who *really* need them, and they try to get by alone or with the support of neighbours.

If your elderly loved one's situation sounds similar to my mum's, you're someone who really needs support from the aged-care system.

COMMON ELIGIBILITY MISCONCEPTIONS

A misconception I hear about eligibility is family members who are supporting elderly loved ones believe or have been told that because they support their loved one, the older person does not qualify for aged-care services.

This is entirely incorrect.

Eligibility is determined by the ability of the older person to complete activities of daily living independently – simple as that.

If you've had a chance to jump onto the My Aged Care website and use the eligibility checker, you'll see how the questions take you through the amount of support required to maintain an older person with day-to-day tasks, and if you've ticked any of the boxes that indicate some support is required, you'll find the older person is considered eligible.

I often hear self-funded retirees say they don't qualify for aged-care services because they are self-funded.

This statement is also incorrect. Eligibility for aged-care services in Australia is not determined by your income status.

I've had so many older people tell me they are ineligible because someone else has told them that. Self-funded retirees are eligible based on their age and limitations in functional ability, just like aged pensioners. Receiving services may incur a cost for self-funded retirees, but does not affect eligibility.

My Aged Care will ask you the Medicare card number for the older person seeking support, but I've had clients who do not have a Medicare card and who are not Australian citizens.

If you don't have a Medicare card you can still register with My Aged Care, but you'll need to call them rather than complete an online referral. The My Aged Care call centre staff will register you manually within the system, create your online account within My Aged Care and then you'll proceed to an assessment. You're also eligible if you are not an Australian citizen and don't have a Medicare card, but there are different levels of eligibility in these circumstances so it's best to contact My Aged Care and discuss your situation. It's a case-by-case situation.

Registering with My Aged Care will give you an Aged Care ID number, which is your personalised identification number. This number starts with AC, followed by eight digits.

* * *

Eligibility for Commonwealth-subsidised services and support within the aged-care system is inclusive, based on age, being 65 years or older, or for First Nations people, being 50 years or older. Eligibility is dependent on requiring some kind of support to continue living at home. Eligibility is not dependent on your financial situation. And it is also not based on you having a live-in carer. You're also eligible if you are not an Australian citizen and don't have a Medicare card but in this situation a discussion with My Aged Care is often required.

If you've been thinking you need some support in looking after a loved one at home and haven't contact My Aged Care because you've heard from someone that you're not eligible, please disregard this incorrect advice and make contact.

I've supported many hundreds of people to receive services within the aged-care system, and although I've heard from other colleagues and organisations in the industry that once in a while a person is deemed ineligible, I personally haven't been involved with anyone who was declined on eligibility.

CHAPTER 5

HOW TO MAKE A REFERRAL TO MY AGED CARE

Before you even contact My Aged Care and register or refer an older loved one, there's much reflection and preparation that needs to occur.

You've given some thought to the day-to-day tasks your elderly loved one needs assistance with and you've drafted a list. You might be realising that you provide more support for your older loved one than you thought.

It can be a confronting experience.

Having considered the situation and prepared for the initial contact with My Aged Care, you're ready to make the referral and progress to an assessment. I recommend that either the older person themselves or someone close to them who knows them well is the person who should be contacting My Aged Care.

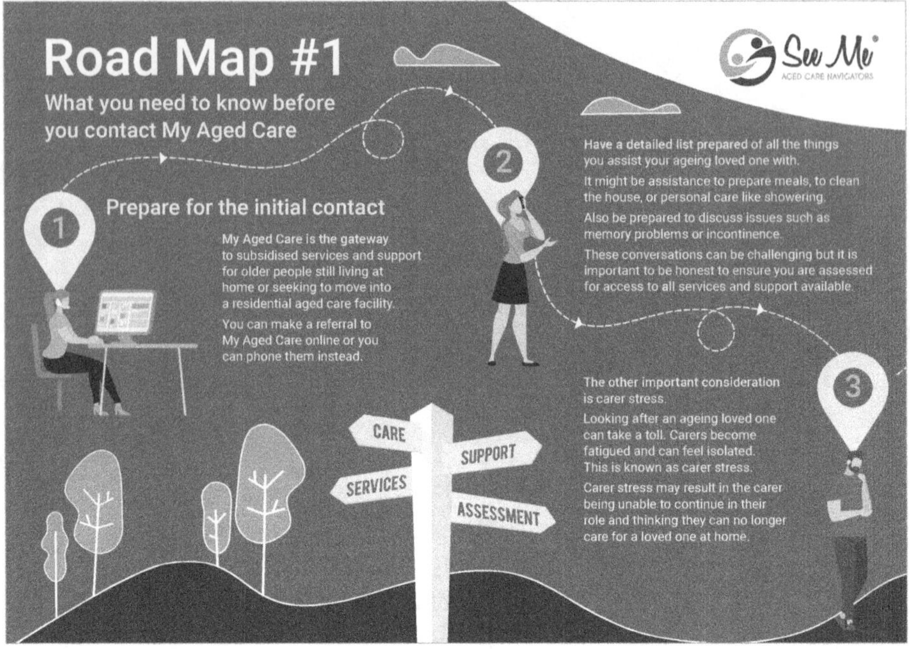

What you need to know before you contact My Aged Care.

MAKING THE REFERRAL FOR YOUR OLDER LOVED ONE

Many clients have said to me that they'll leave it to their GP. I discourage this, and impress upon them why they should be the one to make the referral.

Think about it. Your older loved one might have been seeing their GP for 30 years and believe that the GP knows the older person well. But do they?

In my experience, older people are reluctant to discuss their increasing dependence on their family with their GP, they will not initiate a conversation about continence, and they will be adept at presenting as cognitively intact by answering the doctor's questions appropriately, albeit in very simple responses.

My dad would visit his GP and never raised the issues with his GP that the rest of the family had asked him to raise. Dad was stoic and proud and wanted his GP to think he was capable and managing at home.

I've had clients who are cognitively impaired, some have a diagnosis of dementia, but because they are dressed appropriately and answer the GP's questions seemingly appropriately the GP has no idea what's really going on at home. The GP doesn't know the challenges the person faces each day in regard to shopping for groceries and having enough food in the house, cleaning, taking their medications as prescribed or paying their bills.

And a GP consultation takes all of 15 minutes, maybe 30 minutes if you've managed to book an extended consultation. This amount of time is inadequate to gain a clear picture for the GP to make a robust referral to My Aged Care.

Also, GPs haven't received any education as to how My Aged Care works. Their understanding of the platform and all the programs that sit within community aged care is no more than most people in the community.

Making a well-prepared referral to My Aged Care is integral to ensuring the older person is assessed and approved for the most appropriate programs that will support them to remain at home. You must get this referral right from the initial contact with My Aged Care.

When you're ready to contact My Aged Care and register and make a referral, you have two choices how to do this. You can call My Aged Care, or you can register online.

My advice to anyone who has family nearby is to have a family member sit with the older person when the contact is made or allow the family member to register and make the referral on behalf of the older person.

Consent is essential to the referral proceeding. The older person is likely to be asked by the staff at My Aged Care if they consent to the referral being made and will expect you to hand the phone to the older person to confirm their consent.

When making a referral to My Aged Care, you'll also need to supply the Medicare number of the person being assessed. If the person seeking the assessment doesn't have a Medicare card, a phone referral is the only option as you'll need to explain to the call centre staff why there is no Medicare card and they will register the person manually.

Ensure you've put aside some time to make this referral. Ensure there won't be any distractions or background noise. If you choose to make an online referral and become distracted and leave the site for some time, the referral will time out and you'll need to start again.

Making a referral to My Aged Care is *not* the assessment. The My Aged Care call centre staff are not assessors. The call centre staff ask a series of generic questions and then, based on your answers to these generic questions, they'll forward the referral to one of two assessment teams.

Making the referral to My Aged Care is only the first step in a series of steps that involve assessment, approval and, finally, assignment of the support you are seeking.

The call centre staff at My Aged Care have varying knowledge and experience in the aged-care sector. They are not a workforce who have been working in aged care previously, though there may be individuals who have had previous experience in the industry.

Because of the varying knowledge and experience, the person you speak to at My Aged Care may not be familiar with all the programs available nor the eligibility for these programs.

I have had many conversations with different staff at the call centre, particularly regarding the Short-Term Restorative Care (STRC) program. The conversations that involve a referral for STRC often begin with the My Aged Care call centre staff telling me a person is not presenting as needing an assessment by the ACAT.

STRC is a re-ablement program, led by clinicians, with the goal of the program being to enable an older person to restore their independence to place them in the best position to continue living at home.

Because the screening process for a My Aged Care referral fails to adequately capture a person's situation, a person who is eligible for STRC may also look like someone with basic needs who would also sit appropriately within the entry-level program, the Commonwealth Home Support Programme (CHSP).

But only the ACAT can approve a person for STRC. So a person who is eligible for and who would benefit from a program of restorative care could be denied approval for the program because the call centre staff are unfamiliar with it.

Being familiar with all the programs offered for community-focused aged care enables you, the referrer, to discuss and advise the My Aged Call centre staff on what might be appropriate for your older loved one.

Stepping off on the right foot and placing yourself or your older loved one in the best position for the appropriate assessment and subsequent approvals necessitates you understanding your situation in detail and having a thorough understanding of the range of programs offered to support your loved one at home.

Take the time to research and reflect.

Take the time to write your list.

And make the time to focus on your discussion or online referral when you're ready to contact My Aged Care.

When you've made contact and are having the discussion, take notes. Write down the points you've discussed with the call centre staff. Note any reference numbers, especially the Aged Care ID number.

I recommend to all my clients to appoint a representative in My Aged Care. I am my mum's representative. This means your older loved one must inform the My Aged Care staff that you can speak on their behalf during the process.

Why? Because this process of registering, referring, receiving an assessment, accepting in-home support and understanding what comes next is complex and confusing, and building the support network starts here. Sharing the information with someone they trust and who is willing to speak on their behalf will be a great benefit to your older loved one.

This is discussed in detail in the following chapter.

HAVING A CLINICIAN MAKE THE REFERRAL

The other option for making a referral is via a clinician, including GPs and other medical professionals, such as a geriatrician. Having said GPs are not best placed to make the referral to My Aged Care on your or your elderly loved one's behalf, there can be a benefit to having a GP or other clinician make the referral as the clinician referral platform allows for greater detail to be offered regarding a person's presentation.

Having your loved one's GP or geriatrician make the referral to My Aged Care doesn't guarantee that the referral will be received at the ACAT though, which is unfortunately what many GPs and geriatricians believe. The authority of the GP or geriatrician in this context of health provision carries no additional influence that a person needs coordinated support instead of fragmented and entry-level support.

A clinician referral to My Aged Care provides additional options for demonstrating a person's deficits in their day-to-day activities. The view that I see when I'm accessing the My Aged Care website, which is the view that other clinicians see, allows for more detailed input to explain a person's situation compared to if you do it your-self. It also allows for uploading of up to three documents to provide additional details.

When I'm making an online referral for a client, I upload my comprehensive assessment and another two screening tools I've used that clearly show why I am seeking the kind of assessment I am. I might upload a functional screening tool and a screening tool that relates to cognition, mood or carer stress.

I add as much information as I can, conveying why I am seeking a certain assessment.

Reflecting that the call centre staff at My Aged Care may not be familiar with all the programs available to older people living at home, I describe the person's functional limitations and goals that align with a program of restorative care if I'm seeking an assessment for STRC for my client.

* * *

The intent of making a referral to My Aged Care is the same, no matter if you choose to make the referral on behalf of your elderly loved one, or you allow your GP, geriatrician or other clinician to do this.

Whoever makes the referral needs to understand the process well and support the referral with a clear and comprehensive account of the elderly person's situation.

Now let's take a closer look at My Aged Care representatives.

CHAPTER 6
APPOINTING A MY AGED CARE REPRESENTATIVE

Registering with My Aged Care, progressing through the assessments and approvals, understanding what an approved referral code means, knowing how to go about sourcing services related to a referral code and knowing how to choose a great provider for a Home Care Package is a complex and lengthy process.

This process isn't intuitive, and may involve many re-referrals, reassessments, a need for adjusted approvals and possibly moving from one provider to another. Communication is vital to ensure these processes occur as they should, in a timely manner and so they reflect the changing needs of the older person.

WHY REPRESENTATIVES ARE IMPORTANT

Appointing a representative in My Aged Care shares the tasks of communication and action. Having someone to support an older loved one, to speak on their behalf and to advocate for them when things aren't going well, is imperative to achieving better outcomes within the system.

Appointing a representative within My Aged Care is not a legal obligation nor is it concerned with managing finances or health decisions. Appointing a representative within My Aged Care is solely for the purpose of efficient and effective communication at each step in the journey. Appointing a representative in My Aged Care ensures the older person doesn't fall through the cracks of this very complex and fragmented system.

The older people who fall through the cracks of the system tend to be those who are not connected by email or who don't use the internet. They are also people who live some distance from family members. And they are the people who are somewhat disconnected from their community; that is, they may not see their GP regularly, they have stopped attending community groups and have become isolated from friends. They are also people who have emerging cognitive impairment but are still presenting as managing at home.

The older people who fall through the cracks of the system are also the cohort who have an understanding of scammers and have been advised by their family not to agree to anything when someone calls them on the phone. These are the people who aren't referred to My Aged Care until a crisis happens and they end up in hospital and the treating team decides they cannot go home. No one has been aware that they are struggling to manage at home.

Having at least one representative within My Aged Care increases the chances of the older person having more timely and personalised interactions with assessment teams and service providers. A My Aged Care representative can speak on an older person's behalf, being the point of contact and making decisions in support of an older person's choices.

The representative will also receive any documentation from My Aged Care that relates to approvals for care. Should the older person want more than one representative appointed, this is possible.

Representatives will also be given a unique registration number and will need to quote this number when contacting My Aged Care on their loved one's behalf.

THE TYPES OF REPRESENTATIVES

There are two types of representatives within My Aged Care.

One is a 'regular representative', and the other is an 'authorised representative'.

A regular representative can be appointed by the older person by speaking with the My Aged Care call centre staff or when an online referral to My Aged Care is made. Or if the older person is already registered with My Aged Care, someone can download and print the 'Appointment of a Representative' form.

When completed, this form needs to be faxed or mailed back to My Aged Care. The person seeking to be a representative will also need to supply their Medicare card details.

Another option is during an assessment: the older person can ask the assessor to note the details of the person being appointed, to be uploaded to My Aged Care on completion of the assessment.

A regular representative is not a legally appointed substitute decision maker for the older person. The legally appointed decision maker is the second option, the authorised representative.

Appointing an authorised representative follows the same process as a regular representative but requires legal documentation to validate the appointment. An authorised representative is usually appointed when the older person is deemed unable to make decisions or act for themself.

The legal documentation required varies from state to state and territory and may include:

- a guardianship order
- an enduring guardian document and a letter from a doctor stating the older person cannot act on their own behalf
- an enduring power of attorney document and a letter from a doctor stating the older person cannot act on their own behalf.

If you don't have any of these documents and want to be appointed as an authorised representative, you'll need to supply My Aged Care with a statutory declaration stating you are the most appropriate person to represent the older person and you'll also need a letter from a doctor stating the older person is unable to act for themself.

In my experience, older people who have My Aged Care representatives achieve timelier and more appropriate outcomes, and they don't fall through the cracks because the representative is regularly monitoring and following up on behalf of the older person.

WHO SHOULD BE A REPRESENTATIVE?

Who is the most appropriate person or persons to be appointed as a representative within My Aged Care?

For a regular representative, it's not necessarily the legally appointed substitute decision maker, not in this instance.

The most appropriate person to be representing an older person within My Aged Care is the person who fulfils the caregiving role. It's the person who has a thorough understanding of the day-to-day limitations and needs of the older person.

Why would it not be the legally appointed substitute decision maker in this instance?

Because communication with My Aged Care needs to detail those day-to-day limitations and needs. The representative should be the person who can convey to My Aged Care, to assessment teams and to home care providers – in great detail – what the older person needs to enable them to remain living at home.

The detail concerns how much assistance the older person needs to maintain a clean home, if they need someone to help them shower, if they need someone to do the grocery shopping or prepare meals for them, if the older person is dependent on someone arranging their appointments and transporting them.

Confirming consent to appoint a representative

I had a client, the daughter of an older lady.

The daughter lived in a different state to her mum.

The daughter contacted me to discuss how the aged-care system works and what she should be thinking about to engage services and support for her mum, who lived alone.

The daughter made an online referral to My Aged Care for her mum and noted that she was to be the primary contact for her.

The daughter felt her mum wouldn't be able to understand all the terminology and the steps involved in registering for, being assessed for and eventually choosing a provider for support at home.

But at this stage the daughter couldn't arrange to be the representative as the My Aged Care staff had to confirm consent with the older lady to have her daughter appointed as the representative.

The My Aged Care staff phoned the daughter after the referral was completed online to discuss the referral, namely why she had noted she was to be the primary contact and not her mother. The daughter explained what the situation was and asked the My Aged Care staff to call the mum and gain consent, which they did.

When the consent was noted and the daughter was registered as her mum's representative, the daughter was able to discuss her mum's situation on her behalf, presenting the circumstances at home in detail and urging the My Aged Care staff to progress the referral to the ACAT for a specific program.

The daughter was able to articulate her mum's needs better than her mum could have and was able to position her mum for an assessment and approvals that reflected her needs.

* * *

Appointing a representative in My Aged Care is important. A representative is acknowledged by the staff at My Aged Care as having the consent to speak on behalf of an older person and information from My Aged Care will be shared willingly.

A My Aged Care representative does not fulfil the same role as a legally appointed substitute decision maker. A My Aged Care representative is not concerned in this instance with financial, health or lifestyle decisions; the appointment is only to facilitate efficient and effective communication within the aged-care system.

Without an appointed My Aged Care representative formally noted within the system, the staff at My Aged Care will not discuss or disclose any details about the older person.

Leaving an older person to fend for themself within the aged-care system is fraught with peril and may disadvantage them in communication and decision making. When the initial conversations are happening, agreeing on and appointing the most appropriate caregiver as the representative in My Aged Care will ensure better outcomes as the older person moves through the system.

Being a regular representative has no alignment with being a legally appointed substitute decision maker. But to be an authorised representative, you need to produce the documents, an enduring power of attorney, and also demonstrate impaired decision making capacity with a doctor's letter. This negates consent as you are now regarded as the decision maker.

A regular representative is not a legally appointed substitute decision maker – an enduring power of attorney – and this nomination by the older person requires their consent.

An authorised representative negates consent as this recognises the older person as not having decision making capacity and the substitute decision maker is enacted by having the legal documentation and a doctor's letter stating the older person cannot make their own decisions.

CHAPTER 7
WHAT HAPPENS NEXT?

Taking the time to understand what a referral means, how to present a dialogue that is thorough and detailed, and being ready to step up and advocate for your older loved one in these initial stages is just the beginning of an ongoing process.

You've taken the time to discuss formal support with your older loved one, you've created a list of all the support your older loved one is receiving from family, friends or neighbours, and you've registered your older loved one within My Aged Care.

What happens next?

IMMEDIATELY AFTER YOUR REFERRAL

After you've called My Aged Care or made an online referral, you wait.

That's right, you wait.

If you've made an online referral, staff from My Aged Care may call you and discuss further with you what your older loved one's needs are. Remember, My Aged Care is not the assessment team.

My Aged Care is the registration and screening phase and the conduit to reach one of the two assessment teams.

Based on the information you've supplied when registering or referring to My Aged Care, the referral will be forwarded to the Regional Assessment Service (RAS) or the Aged Care Assessment Team (ACAT), or in Victoria, the Aged Care Assessment Service (ACAS).

These are the two assessment services.

Both the RAS and the ACAT have prescribed timelines for which initial contact must be made with the client. The initial contact from the RAS or ACAT assessor usually confirms some details and then, in discussion with the older person or their representative, a date and time will be made to undertake the assessment.

Prior to Covid 19, assessments were completed at a person's home. Since Covid 19, many assessment teams, both RAS and ACATs, are now assessing over the phone.

A phone assessment isn't ideal as a lot of information can be missed, hence it is important you've given thought to your loved one's situation so you can be clear with the assessor about what is really going on at home.

The assessor may or may not tell you which assessment team they are from when they make initial contact, so it's advisable to ask them and note this information. Many people incorrectly assume they are being assessed by the ACAT, when in fact their details have been progressed to the RAS. People often think that My Aged Care is the ACAT too.

Assessment teams have their own triaging processes, and assessments coming via the My Aged Care portal are triaged once they are received by the RAS or the ACAT. Priority, that is urgency for assessment, will tend to push a referral to the forefront, particularly for the ACAT assessments. Priority for an assessment is indicated by a situation of risk. The risk being the older person may be admitted prematurely to an aged-care facility or to hospital if services and support cannot be commenced within the home urgently. This situation is specifically relevant to carer crisis; that is, the spouse or family member of the older person is so exhausted that they feel they are unable to continue to care for their loved one, even though they want to.

Waiting for an assessment is dependent on many factors, and may include the urgency identified in the screening and subsequent triage process, the availability of staff in the RAS and ACAT in any given local area and the number of referrals already waiting for assessors. ACAT assessors cover large geographical areas, and if travel is required for face-to-face assessments this can also increase wait times.

FOLLOWING UP YOUR REFERRAL

My advice to older people and their family is that if they haven't heard from an assessment team within three weeks, to call My Aged Care and ask where the referral has been sent, but it may take longer before an assessment team has made contact with you or your older loved one.

If you've been appointed as the representative, My Aged Care will give you this information. If you are not noted as a representative, My Aged care will not disclose this information to you.

While you're waiting for the assessment to happen, continue to keep notes on what is going on in the day-to-day life of the older person awaiting the assessment. Sometimes during this waiting period, the situation at home may deteriorate quickly or the person caring for the older loved one may not be able to continue in their caring role.

It's important to act quickly in these situations and alert My Aged Care to the changing needs at home. A situation of urgency may allow an assessor to prioritise an assessment as there is a recognition of increasing risk. A situation of urgency may be a rapid decline in function due to an incident such as a fall, or it may be that the carer cannot continue to support the older person anymore and the only option for care may be with a hospital admission.

* * *

The key takeaway message in this chapter is, don't wait for an extended period of time to be contacted by an assessment team, especially if your older loved one has deteriorated since the referral occurred.

I've known of many older people who have been referred via My Aged Care for an assessment by a family member or a discharge planner in a hospital, and when My Aged Care calls the older person to discuss the referral or the ACAT calls the older person to schedule the assessment, the older person tells them they are fine and the referral is then 'deactivated'. And that's that. My Aged Care doesn't notify you that your older loved one has declined an assessment and your older loved one has fallen through the first crack.

It's important to follow up and ensure the process is progressing as it should.

If the RAS assessor or ACAT assessor has contacted you or your older loved one but not scheduled an assessment date yet and there is a sudden change for the worse in the situation, call the assessor back and convey the deteriorating circumstances.

Once contact has been made by the RAS or ACAT assessor, they usually give their phone number. With the ACAT, there is usually a generic number you can call to expedite the assessment if necessary.

If you've invested the time and effort to prepare for a referral to My Aged Care, maintain the momentum and follow through with ensuring the referral reaches an assessment team. Then use the waiting time wisely to keep monitoring your older loved one, gathering any additional information that might be helpful to an assessor, such as medical summaries or reports from specialists, and position yourself to present a detailed and compelling conversation with the assessing team member.

PART II

RECEIVING ENTRY-LEVEL SUPPORT

WHERE DO I START?
AM I ELIGIBLE?
WHAT HAPPENS NEXT?

CHAPTER 8
WHAT IS THE COMMONWEALTH HOME SUPPORT PROGRAMME?

The Commonwealth Home Support Programme (CHSP) is the entry-level funding stream that offers people the opportunity to receive services and support in their home. CHSP-funded services are often the first type of Government-subsidised support that people entering the aged-care system receive.

The Commonwealth Home Support Programme was launched in July 2015 and consolidated four services:

- the Commonwealth Home and Community Care (HACC) program
- the National Respite for Carers Program (NRCP)
- the Day Therapy Centres (DTC) program
- the Assistance with Care and Housing for the Aged (ACHA) program.

Being the entry-level program, the amount of support or services that a person can receive is limited. The funding from the government is of course finite, and once granted can only be spread across so many people until it's exhausted.

CHSP-FUNDED SERVICES

CHSP-funded services include:

- domestic assistance
- personal care assistance
- yard maintenance
- social support
- meals
- nursing and allied health
- home modifications.

CHSP also funds respite care, but not the respite that people access in an aged-care facility or nursing home.

The amount of support or services someone receives is related to the number of approvals received from their assessment. More on the assessment and approvals in the next chapter.

CHSP services are typically fragmented; that is, any service or support a person receives at home from their approved referral codes may be delivered by any number of service providers. These CHSP services may be offered as 'once off', intermittently or ongoing.

CHSP services will cease if a person accepts a Home Care Package, as accessing both these programs – the CHSP and the Home Care Package program – at the same time is regarded as 'double dipping', except in some exceptional circumstances.

Given this type of funding needs to be stretched to meet the needs of many older people living at home, the dollar value attached to certain types of CHSP services continually decreases as providers try to make the funding stretch as far as possible.

Trying to make the money last

A CHSP provider of home maintenance in my local area was allocating $600 per person per year for minor home modifications three years ago.

This amount now sits at $350 per year per person.

This provider is trying to make the funding for home maintenance stretch across as many people needing maintenance in their homes as possible.

The CHSP manual 2020–22 describes the amount of service a person receives under this program as not exceeding the dollar value of funding that someone would receive from a Home Care Package level 1.

The dollar value the manual details for CHSP-funded services or support a person should receive is $8000 pa. Just to be clear, that $8000 is the funding amount that is being subsidised by the government that is allocated to a provider to deliver CHSP services. For example, I've had clients who are receiving CHSP-funded personal care five days per week and registered nursing support three days per week as well. These clients had complex needs that required a registered nurse to attend to wound care and complex continence issues.

In this particular case, this amount of CHSP support would exceed $8000 over one year. Given the guidelines in the manual, these clients should be receiving a high-level Home Care Packages instead, to provide that high level of personal and clinical support.

If someone is using CHSP-funded services and support that exceed this amount, the CHSP provider should be reviewing the individual's situation and thinking about referring them to the ACAT for an assessment for a Home Care Package.

WHO IS ELIGIBLE FOR CHSP SERVICES AND SUPPORT?

Eligibility for this program aligns with the eligibility criteria as detailed on the My Aged Care website, being people from 65 years and older or First Nations people aged 50 and over.

There are also extenuating circumstances for people at risk of homelessness to access CHSP-funded services, and the age criteria is lowered to people being 50 years or older and are prematurely aged or are on a low income or are 45 years or older for First Nations people. The key point here is being homeless or at risk of being homeless.

CHSP-funded services and support are available to people who are not Australian citizens or permanent residents of Australia. What this means is that if you or your older loved one do not have a Medicare card, you should not let this stop you from contacting My Aged Care and discussing your situation.

The growth of culturally appropriate service providers also has increased the ability to support and advocate for people who don't realise they are eligible to receive CHSP-funded services and support.

Diversity is also recognised within CHSP, underpinned by the *Aged Care Act 1997*. This program ensures older people with specific social, cultural, linguistic, religious, spiritual, psychological, medical and care needs are included in specifically aligned services. CHSP recognises the following special needs groups:

- people who identify as Aboriginal and Torres Strait Islander
- people from culturally and linguistically diverse backgrounds
- people who live in rural and remote areas
- people who are financially or socially disadvantaged
- people who are veterans of the Australian Defence Force or an allied defence force, including the spouse, widow or widower of a veteran
- people who are homeless, or at risk of becoming homeless
- people who are lesbian, gay, bisexual, transgender, intersex and queer
- people who are Care Leavers (which includes Forgotten Australians, Former Child Migrants and Stolen Generations)
- parents separated from children by forced adoption or removal.

CHSP also recognises that the above list is not exhaustive and other special needs groups exist, such as people with a disability, people with mental illness and people living with cognitive impairment.

CHSP also considers supporting people in correctional centres and detention facilities where these services are not already provided by these institutions.

HOW MUCH FUNDING IS AVAILABLE?

Given the extensive list of people who are eligible for CHSP-funded services, how much funding has been provided by the government and how many people are accessing the CHSP for support?

The most recent report commissioned for the Commonwealth Government by Deloitte Access Economics (in October 2020) reviewed data from the period 2018–19 and noted funding as being $2.4 billion. The Department of Health puts this figure at $2.5 billion for the same period.

The number of people reported to have received CHSP services during this timeframe was 840,984, accounting for nearly two-thirds of all aged-care clients. And 534,117 of these older people lived in major cities, 290,716 lived in regional areas and 15,911 lived in remote areas. At the end of 2021, 825,383 older Australians had received support from CHSP.[1]

CHSP funding has been extended by the government as we move towards the implementation of reforms in July 2023 – after this time, under the new Support at Home Program, CHSP services and support will be merged into this new model.

How does this relate to you, the reader of this book? Until the Support at Home Program is implemented in 2023, CHSP-funded support is available to older people living at home. So, let's take a look now at who assesses and approves for the CHSP.

---

1   Commonwealth Home Support Programme Data Study (health.gov.au),
      www.gen-agedcaredata.gov.au/www_aihwgen/media/DoH-factsheets/CHSP-Fact-
      Sheet-2018-19.pdf?ext=.pdf
      www.health.gov.au/sites/default/files/documents/2022/04/budget-2022-23-home-care-
      supporting-senior-australians-to-remain-independent-for-longer.pdf.

CHAPTER 9

WHAT IS THE REGIONAL ASSESSMENT SERVICE?

The Regional Assessment Services (RAS, pronounced 'raz') workforce undertake a 'home support assessment' and approve older people for services and support under the CHSP. RAS assessors are employed by a variety of organisations, which receive Commonwealth funding to manage this workforce. Uniquely, in Victoria, the State Health Department receives this funding and RAS assessments in Victoria are completed by a workforce that falls under the state public health system. These organisations are not necessarily located within the same region as the clients they assess; RAS assessors may be flown in from larger cities to regional towns to complete assessments.[1]

RAS assessors can be the first assessment team older people are attended by, and the distinction between RAS and the ACAT is an important one. We'll discuss the ACAT in greater detail in chapter 14.

---

1   The organisations that are currently receiving government funding to complete RAS assessments are listed here: www.health.gov.au/sites/default/files/documents/2021/09/ regional-assessment-service-organisations-by-state-and-territory-and-region_0.pdf.

RAS assessors are not usually clinicians. They are vocationally trained, and their scope of knowledge with older person care and with services and support available locally is limited. In my experience, many RAS assessors are also unfamiliar with the range of options available within the aged-care system. It has implications for people who have complex needs or who may benefit from a program of reablement – such as Short-Term Restorative Care – if the RAS assessor is unaware of these programs and doesn't forward their referral to the Aged Care Assessment Team. And worse, I've had clients who were deemed ineligible by the RAS assessor for an ACAT assessment because they had live-in carers providing support to the older loved one.

A RAS assessment

A daughter of an older lady contacted me for advice about the aged-care system. She wanted to understand RAS and ACAT assessments and be informed about what the approvals meant from each assessment team.

The older lady was cognitively impaired but functionally okay. But the risk of this older lady living at home was that as her cognition deteriorated, she wouldn't be able to manage her activities of daily living safely. The older lady didn't have insight into her impaired cognition and was resistant to receiving support.

I met with the daughter and her mum and we adopted a gentle approach that considered CHSP services to be the most appropriate way to introduce help, with yard maintenance and social support.

The lawn-mowing contractor wouldn't need to come into her home, and social support was introduced as being a friend dropping over for a cuppa.

The daughter was system literate, so armed with the necessary knowledge, she felt comfortable to progress to the next steps. She made the referral to My Aged Care herself.

The daughter contacted me much sooner than expected to advise a RAS assessor had assessed her mum on the Saturday. I had seen them on Thursday.

The daughter explained that the RAS assessor was in town, having flown up from the major city for a few days to complete assessments as there were no local RAS assessors. The RAS assessor was squeezing this assessment in before she had to catch the plane home.

In following up with me, the daughter then had 101 questions about 'what happens next'.

The RAS assessor had completed her assessment but hadn't had time to explain to the daughter what would happen next. The RAS assessor hadn't explained the referral codes (approvals to receive services under CHSP), or that she would forward these referral codes to local CHSP providers.

Not being based locally, the RAS assessor was also unable to discuss with the daughter who and how local CHSP providers offered services, if there was a waitlist or if these providers were at capacity and have closed their portal. The portal is the pathway inside My Aged Care where providers can see approvals and accept or decline these approvals. Some providers will close their portal if they are at capacity and cannot take on any more clients. Clients don't know this; they think they have been referred for services, but they never hear from the provider telling them they cannot be accepted for that support.

In this instance, when we got to the bottom of it, the referral code for yard maintenance had not been accepted by *the only provider in town* to offer lawn mowing under CHSP. That provider was at capacity and not accepting new approvals.

The social support also did not eventuate as the provider had a long waitlist and couldn't offer any support workers in the foreseeable future.

HOW DOES THE ASSESSMENT WORK?

RAS assessors use an assessment tool, the National Screening and Assessment Form (NSAF), to assess people. This form follows the same format used by the My Aged Care call centre staff. The NSAF gathers personal information about an older person, considers the location where the older person is assessed and if information was sought from anyone else.

The assessment process then delves into the circumstances triggering the assessment and begins to cover the domains that demonstrate where an older person has limitations in their ability to manage their activities of daily living and where they need support. This includes the social domain: family and community engagement and support. It also considers the role of the carer, or if the person being assessed is the carer for someone else. The sustainability of the role of the carer is assessed within this domain too.

The physical domain is assessed. RAS assessors may observe a person moving around their home, noting any difficulty getting up from a chair or how balanced they are when walking. Or they may not. If they don't observe your loved one moving about their home, you will need to be clear with the assessor about any functional limitations, impaired mobility, falls and what day-to-day activities they need assistance with.

The RAS assessor should ideally also ask about pain, continence and cognition.

And they should also ask about carer stress.

But mostly they don't – not in my experience.

Why don't RAS assessors ask about these important issues? Because they are not clinicians and don't recognise signs such as if an older person was just getting out of bed when the RAS assessor arrived, if they reported not needing breakfast as they weren't hungry and were answering questions with as little detail as possible. An experienced clinician would begin to wonder if this older person was experiencing a mood disorder or cognitive impairment, or both.

RAS assessors are trained to assess people who present at 'entry level', so expecting them to fully understand what they are seeing, or not seeing, is probably unrealistic. I accept that, but key in this situation is that – when needed – the RAS assessor acknowledges that something is beyond their scope and refers on to the ACAT for a comprehensive assessment.

* * *

It is vital you take a proactive role in accurately relaying your situation to the RAS assessor. *Your* preparation and ability to articulate your loved one's needs in detail will ensure the RAS assessor has a thorough understanding of your circumstances and approve all the necessary CHSP services or refer on to the ACAT.

CHAPTER 10

WHAT SERVICES ARE AVAILABLE UNDER CHSP?

Older people who have received approvals – known as 'referral codes' – from a RAS assessment may receive one or two, or many, services that are funded under CHSP.

CHSP services are broad but also specific.[1]

Domestic assistance may include house cleaning, helping someone with their laundry tasks or doing a person's grocery shopping for them.

Social support may be provided as individual support or group support. Individual support may be receiving a visit from a support worker or going out for a coffee with a support worker, or even a phone call check-in from a provider. Group social support may be attending activities at a centre-based group.

---

1   For a detailed list of all CHSP services, go to: www.health.gov.au/sites/default/files/documents/2019/12/commonwealth-home-support-programme-chsp-service-catalogue_0.pdf.

Transport might be offered as a bus pick up and drop off service around the local area, or a provider may issue the older person with taxi vouchers.

Home maintenance might be garden maintenance or home maintenance and repairs.

RAS VERSUS ACAT APPROVALS FOR CHSP SERVICES

For the sake of this discussion, I just want to point out that ACAT assessors can also approve CHSP-funded services. I'm raising this here as the CHSP-funded services that the ACAT approves may have a different orientation than the services a RAS assessor approves.

I'll explain.

CHSP-funded services that the RAS generally approve are:

- domestic assistance
- social support
- transport
- home maintenance
- meals
- personal care
- centre-based respite.

When the ACAT approve CHSP services, these services may include the abovementioned services but will also consider clinically orientated support such as nursing support for wound care or continence assessments, physio or exercise physiologist–led group exercise programs, occupational therapist assessments, dieticians, speech pathologists and podiatry and specialised support such as dementia advisor support.

ACATs, being clinicians, are looking to refer to clinical services to support older people at home. Clinician support under CHSP funding could involve almost any clinical professional, dependent again on the type of CHSP funding the provider has been allocated. Some CHSP providers have the ability to offer nursing services and some don't. Some CHSP providers have the ability to offer occupational therapist assessments and some don't.

In my local area, there are three CHSP providers who offer nursing support. There are two CHSP providers who offer assessments with an occupational therapist, two of these are the same ones who offer nursing support. One CHSP provider offers speech pathology.

The point to note here is that clinical support under CHSP funding is always in high demand, so providers who are allocated funding to deliver clinical support under CHSP funding tend to have significant waitlists, or if the service or funding is maxed out, they might 'close their books', essentially meaning they'll close their portal or decline approvals via My Aged Care for new clients seeking such services.

A COMMON TRAP TO AVOID

Providers of CHSP-funded services may also be providers of Home Care Packages. This distinction is important to understand as many older people and their families and carers don't realise that there *isn't* an overlap or duplication of support. Many older people, their families and carers think that the service or support that's received from a CHSP provider naturally becomes the responsibility of that same provider when the person is assigned their Home Care Package. It doesn't.

Questionable practices by a provider

I was involved with a client who was receiving another type of government-funded program, Short-Term Restorative Care (STRC, more on this program in chapter 14).

This client was receiving CHSP domestic support at the same time as receiving STRC. Unlike other programs, a person can still receive their CHSP services while also receiving STRC.

I went to my client's home one day and she was very agitated. She told me that the previous day, a lady had come about her cleaning, wanting her to sign something to continue with her CHSP cleaning. My alarm bells began to ring.

My client went on to tell me that this lady also said, 'When your package with the other provider finishes, we will take over'.

My alarm bells were clanging loudly now.

I realised that the lady was talking about a Home Care Package and was suggesting, or rather telling, my client that they were going to deliver her Home Care Package.

I asked my client if she had received a letter advising her she had been assigned a Home Care Package. She said she had not.

Let me explain everything that is wrong with this situation and how this type of situation occurs. It might get a little convoluted but bear with me; this is *very* important to understand.

Firstly, how did the provider of the CHSP services know that my client had been assigned a Home Care Package before my client was informed?

Simple, because organisations who offer CHSP services get to see the activity in the My Aged Care portal, and when a Home Care Package is assigned to a person, they get to see this instantly.

The recipient has to wait for a letter to be issued by My Aged Care telling them they have been assigned a Home Care Package.

The person assigned a Home Care Package can often be the last person to know if they rely only on information being physically delivered to their letterbox. The client is disadvantaged from this point.

Fortunately, my client still had three weeks remaining on her STRC package, which bought us time to get things sorted.

A person cannot receive an STRC and a Home Care Package at the same time, so while the lady from the CHSP/HCP provider had signed my client up to deliver her Home Care Package, this couldn't come into effect until the STRC program concluded.

My client is a very independent lady and likes to make her own decisions and choose how and who she will engage to support her at home; she was upset that she was being denied choice in who was going to provide an ongoing service under her Home Care Package. My client had a private arrangement with a local gent who mowed her lawn, and she wanted to maintain that arrangement when she accepted her Home Care Package.

The lady who came from the CHSP/HCP provider told my client she would provide her lawn mowing and cleaning and it wouldn't cost her anything. My alarm bells were ringing very loudly by this stage.

I asked my client if she had signed anything. At first, she wasn't sure, then she told me she signed 'one of those things that kids draw on, like a screen that you can wipe away the drawing'.

I knew that what she was referring to was a tablet. My client had signed with this CHSP provider to deliver her Home Care Package, and she had no idea that this is what she had done.

My client was very upset. She said the lady was very pushy, that the lady had wandered in and out of the bedrooms, and that the lady was telling her what was going to happen. I sat down with my client and explained the situation and how I could assist her to make it right.

We discussed consumer-directed care, we discussed choice, we discussed the Charter of Rights, and we made a plan to get the CHSP provider to release the Home Care Package so my client could make the choice herself as to who she wanted to sign with.

I phoned the CHSP provider when I returned to the office, asking to speak with the coordinator who had signed my client up. The person I was speaking to was in the head office in the capital city. This person asked if they could help me, so I began to explain the situation and again asked to be put through to the local coordinator who signed my client up for her Home Care Package. The person at head office told me the local coordinator was unavailable but that she would pass on a message so the coordinator could return my call.

I waited for that call. And I waited. Then I called head office again, explaining that what the coordinator had done was not okay and requesting on my client's behalf to be released from the Home Care Package she had inadvertently signed up for.

At this point I was told that was not possible and that further communication was also not possible because I was not nominated as a representative with the CHSP provider for my client. So, I went back to my client's home and we called the CHSP provider together, or rather my client called them and I sat next to her to provide support.

We put the phone on speaker and I recorded the conversation.

My client got the runaround. The CHSP receptionist told her he couldn't release the Home Care Package, that the local coordinator (who I still had not spoken with) needed to discuss this with my client. So my client asked to be put through to the local coordinator.

The CHSP receptionist came back and said the coordinator was unavailable that day, that she only worked part-time. My client asked to speak with someone else. She said she wanted this issue sorted today. My client was put on hold. And she waited. She waited 16 minutes on hold. Then the CHSP receptionist came back and said the other person he was trying to reach was also not available.

By this time my client was really annoyed, understandably, and told the receptionist again she wanted her Home Care Package released by the CHSP provider and wanted it done today. The receptionist eventually said he would release the package.

My client again confirmed, 'You *will* release it today, won't you ... ' to which he answered 'yes' and then thanked my client for calling.

We were gobsmacked. We sat there staring at each other trying to comprehend what had just happened.

The following week, at my next visit with my client, I contacted the ACAT, seeking confirmation that the Home Care Package had been released from the CHSP provider so my client could approach her preferred provider.

The ACAT advised us that it appeared the Home Care Package was still 'accepted' by the CHSP provider. My client then called My Aged Care who confirmed this also.

My client made another call to the CHSP provider, was connected to the local coordinator this time and demanded her Home Care Package be released. The local coordinator agreed to release the package. The local coordinator also told my client, 'You will *never* receive services from us again.'

My client waited for a few days, then contacted her preferred Home Care Package provider and asked them if they could see her Home Care Package sitting in the portal. They could, meaning that the CHSP provider had at last released the package.

My client then asked the coordinator of her preferred provider to come out to her home so she could sign up with them.

This situation I've just described is way too common. CHSP providers who offer entry-level services get their foot in the door with older people first, to provide those entry-level services to people living at home. There is not much that can be done about this under our present system as this CHSP funding is allocated to a finite number of providers and there isn't much choice in many areas for people to choose their own CHSP provider. The services and support delivered under CHSP funding can be the same type of services and support that would be delivered by a Home Care Package provider, so it is imperative you understand that CHSP funding is allocated to the provider, not the client.

Because people are unaware that the services they receive from CHSP funding may be the services they'll elect to have their Home Care Package funding cover, they think there is a seamless continuity between the two programs.

This is incorrect. CHSP and HCP funding are separate.

CHSP funding is allocated to a provider, leaving very little option for choice about who will deliver such support as cleaning under this program. With Home Care Package funding, the funding is allocated to the person not the provider, so the funding is portable and means that the person can take that allocated funding to the provider of their choice. So an older person could choose from any number of providers to deliver their cleaning when they receive a home care package.

Older people and their carers are often unaware that once the older person is assigned their Home Care Package, they are free to choose their preferred provider.

This is also discussed in chapter 12.

* * *

Let's now take a closer look at who receives CHSP funding. This will help you to successfully navigate the system.

CHAPTER 11

WHO RECEIVES CHSP FUNDING AND WHY IT MATTERS

Even at this entry level, things can become confusing for people entering the aged-care system. Who assesses for what services and who provides this support under CHSP funding is complex right from the start. Complicating things even more is that the CHSP program is going to be merged with Home Care Packages and Short-Term Restorative Care in July 2023. CHSP will not bear any resemblance to the current model under the new Support at Home Program after this.

WHY YOUR CHOICE OF PROVIDER MAY BE LIMITED BY THE FUNDING SYSTEM

But I'll discuss this topic in the final part; for now it's important to understand how the funding is allocated and why your choice of service provider might be limited or you might not receive CHSP-funded services even when you've been approved.

CHSP funding has historically been allocated via grants, via a tendering type of process known as the Aged Care Approvals Round (ACAR). CHSP funding has not been allocated for many years under ACARs, as the government had been moving towards discontinuing CHSP for some time, but kept delaying this until now, as we move towards the new aged-care program, the Support at Home Program.

Because the government has been considering ceasing CHSP for many years, these funding rounds stopped offering CHSP funding for new providers. Providers who have been around for a long time are the only providers who receive CHSP funding.

For example, in my local area, the main CHSP providers are three large faith-based organisations. There are also a few smaller not-for-profit and for-profit organisations that have a lower amount of CHSP funding. The community health facility of my local hospital also has CHSP funding. In Queensland, state health services can receive CHSP funding and deliver CHSP services too. Not all state health services receive CHSP funding, which we'll discuss shortly.

Newer organisations or providers who established themselves in my local area could not apply for CHSP funding under ACARs because this funding is only allocated to existing CHSP providers. This situation was the same everywhere in Australia for any newer organisations who entered the marketplace after the ACARs ceased offering new CHSP funding.

So, who has been allocated CHSP funding around the country? What services or support is offered in your local area that is funded under CHSP?

It's not an easy question to answer.

When the ACARs were offered, not-for-profit, faith-based and for-profit organisations, local councils and state and territory health departments were all vying for a piece of this funding pie.

Some state health departments were allocated large amounts of CHSP funding, such as Queensland and Victoria, and CHSP services are therefore often perceived as being provided by the state health system. The state health system is the service provider for services such as domestic assistance, personal care or clinical support in these instances, but the funding comes from the Federal Government.

Local councils in some states also deliver CHSP services from this type of funding. At present, Victoria's local councils and some local councils in Western Australia, Tasmania and greater Sydney and NSW also deliver CHSP-funded services. However, at the time of writing, some local councils in Victoria are reviewing their ongoing ability to deliver this type of entry-level service under the new Support at Home Program, with many deciding not to continue offering aged-care services to older people living at home, citing increased costs to councils to deliver these services and the need to increase fees to people receiving care.

As the CHSP stands at the time of writing, though, services under CHSP will still be delivered up until July 2023 and the relevant providers are receiving additional funding to carry them through this transition period.

Historically, 'grandfathering'-type arrangements are put in place to ensure people currently receiving services are not disadvantaged when a new aged-care program begins. It is anticipated this type of arrangement will occur for people receiving CHSP services now as we move towards the new approach. No older person should be worse off under the new system.

The My Aged Care website lists providers of CHSP funding in local areas across the country. You can search this feature on the website to find what types of CHSP-funded services are offered in your area, and if the providers specialise in an aspect of older person's care, such as dementia. You can also search based on language and faith.

If searching for a CHSP provider using this function, keep an open mind. How often a provider updates their My Aged Care listing is highly variable, and there are listings from national companies noting they offer support in a local area but in fact they don't.

WHY YOUR SERVICES MAY BE APPROVED BUT NOT DELIVERED

Providers can also display that their service is at capacity and they have a waitlist, meaning you may not receive the CHSP support you have been approved for because the funding has been depleted or there may not be staff available to offer the services displayed in the provider's listing.

It doesn't make it easy for people needing these types of services at home. Getting a RAS assessment, receiving approved referral codes and being told one can get support, but the reality is they may not get support, leaves older people and their families and carers confused and vulnerable.

It's far from fair.

There is no simple answer about what to do in this situation. My advice to people who ask me is 'be the squeaky wheel'. If your older loved one is at risk at home, if they have received referral codes for CHSP services but haven't received any support, call the local CHSP providers and convey your concern and ask to be waitlisted as a priority. Then call My Aged Care and tell them there are no CHSP services available, describe the risk for your older loved one being at home without support and request an ACAT assessment for a Home Care Package.

My Aged Care may not be willing to accept referring onto the ACAT for a Home Care Package assessment but be the squeaky wheel and escalate your concern if necessary. The RAS may contact you again to discuss your older loved one's situation, so be ready to impart this crucial information again, asserting the need for support and requesting an ACAT assessment. The RAS should refer you to the ACAT given the risk. The ACAT will then contact you and discuss your loved one's situation and proceed with an assessment for a Home Care Package or perhaps Short-Term Restorative Care.

* * *

Entering the aged-care system at entry level, having a RAS assessment and being approved for services and support seems like a win for some older people and their families, and it is a win of sorts. But in many instances, this is the point where a person's journey within the system also becomes derailed.

Having an accurate understanding of who is assessing your older loved one, knowing which CHSP provider the RAS is going to forward the approvals to and being aware that a provider should be following up with you or your older loved one is vital to ensure your loved one receives the support needed.

If you know who the provider is that has accepted the referral code, call them and find out if they have capacity to deliver the service your older loved one has been approved for. If the provider does not have capacity, request they release the referral code and phone other CHSP providers in your area and check if they can deliver the approved service.

The code belongs to the person, the CHSP funding belongs to the provider. You can take your referral code to any CHSP provider, but keep in mind, CHSP services are always in high demand, so you might still find you can't receive the services you've been approved for with any other provider as well.

RAS assessors are told that it is easier for them to forward those referral codes to providers on behalf of the person. RAS assessors are also told it is 'fair' to divvy those referral codes out across the range of providers in any local area. Unfortunately they don't tell people this and they don't have any idea that some or all of these CHSP providers have 'closed their books', so the referral codes sit in limbo and no one knows this except the CHSP provider who accepted the referral code from the RAS assessor.

Understanding how the aged-care system works, even at entry level, is imperative to getting services and support in a timely manner.

PART III
RECEIVING COORDINATED HOME SUPPORT

CHAPTER 12
WHAT ARE HOME CARE PACKAGES?

HOW HOME CARE PACKAGES ARE PROVIDED

The next level of home care service provision is the Home Care Packages (HCP) program.

Home Care Packages are allocations of funding, known as a subsidy, that are assigned to the person – *not* the provider as with the Commonwealth Home Support Programme – that allow an older person to receive coordinated services and support at home.

In February 2017 there was a big change in the way older people received a Home Care Package. Prior to this date, providers were assigned the subsidy to deliver these packages, much the same as CHSP is presently funded. The number of Home Care Packages in any given region was static, unless providers received additional funding in each funding round and were able to increase the number of Home Care Packages they were able to deliver. People were approved by the ACAT to receive a Home Care Package, but they had to wait until a provider had a vacancy locally to be offered a package.

There were advantages and disadvantages to this system.

The advantages were that ACAT assessors liaised directly with providers and collaboratively determined priorities for access to the packages, so theoretically a client with urgent needs approved for a package could be offered that package sooner rather than later if the assessor felt the person should be considered more of a priority over other people who had already been waiting for a Home Care Package.

The downside to this system was that the older person didn't have a choice in which provider was going to deliver the package. It also meant that the older person couldn't change package providers as this would mean relinquishing their package and waiting until another provider had a package available.

In 2016 the Federal Government made significant changes in the aged-care industry to enable greater choice and flexibility for consumers. After February 2017, Home Care Packages were assigned to the person. Older people now have a choice in which provider they want take to their Home Care Package to for having their services and support delivered.

Also, because the Home Care Package is assigned to the person and not the provider, packages are considered portable so people can move interstate and still retain the package funding. This also gives people the ability to change package providers if they are dissatisfied with their current provider and feel they could get better service with another provider.

Allocating the subsidy to the person and not the provider was a positive move that allowed people to choose who they wanted to manage their package. It also created some accountability within the industry, as providers who are regarded as being good at supporting their clients attracted other clients who were keen to exercise their choice and move from lacklustre service provision to something better.

Now, I know this might seem a little confusing; I've discussed being able to choose who provides your CHSP-funded services but have stated that CHSP funding sits with a provider. Just to recap, CHSP funding is allocated to a provider. The CHSP referral code or approval belongs to you. Under CHSP, you can take the referral code to any CHSP provider and ask them if they're able to deliver the services aligned with the referral code or approval.

With Home Care Packages, the funding or subsidy is assigned to you, not the provider. The Home Care Package subsidy must still be managed by a provider, but it is your choice who you want as a provider. You're under no obligation to stay with your CHSP provider. This is the benefit of the Home Care Package program; it gives people greater choice as compared with CHSP services.

The growth in the industry over the past few years has resulted in many new providers entering the marketplace and alternative models being offered to clients, such as self-management of their Home Care Package.

THE FOUR LEVELS OF HOME CARE PACKAGES

There are four levels of Home Care Packages, and these reflect the assessed needs of the older person:

- An HCP 1, which is regarded as someone having basic needs.
- An HCP 2, which is regarded as having low care needs.
- An HCP 3, being intermediate needs.
- An HCP 4, being someone who presents with high needs.

Each level of Home Care Package has a designated subsidy aligned with it.

The subsidy for Home Care Packages changes every year on 1 July. At the time of writing, the daily subsidy or funding for a Home Care Package is:

- HCP 1 $25.15 – over a year this is $9179.75.
- HCP 2 $44.24 – over a year this is $16,147.60.
- HCP 3 $96.27 – over a year this is $35,138.55.
- HCP 4 $145.94 – over a year this is $53,268.10.

The subsidy assigned to the level of Home Care Package, while assigned to the older person, is not deposited into their bank account. In providing this funding, the government wants to ensure that the package subsidy is being managed and spent in accordance with the intent of the aged-care program. Reporting of data and demonstrating how funding is spent needs to be undertaken, and this task is delegated to the provider.

The Home Care Package you are assigned is managed by a provider, who accepts responsibility for ensuring standards are upheld and data is collected. For this task the provider will charge you a fee, which is deducted from the subsidy. For example, using a fully managed provider if your older loved one received an HCP 2, they would deduct approximately 30% of the subsidy, leaving your older loved one with a remaining $11,303.32 per annum.

Fully managed providers charge different amounts, but 30% is a common fee across the industry. Some providers charge up to 40% or 50%, and some charge a lot less. Some providers advertise that they charge no fees, but their cost of service delivery, say domestic assistance, is often double.

The allocated subsidy, using an HCP 2 again and being $16,147.60, is not available to you as a lump sum. The subsidy is allocated on a monthly basis.

What this means under the current system is that providers need to discuss with their clients how they want to spend their subsidy each month. If an older person wants to purchase a large item, let's say a mobility scooter, the person would need to forgo something in their package, maybe social support or domestic assistance, and 'save up' for the mobility scooter.

Moving to the new system, Support at Home in 2023, the funding will be allocated differently, and people will potentially be able to access separate funding for these big items and not have to 'save up' for them. The Support at Home Program is being presented as offering 'access to a new program for goods, equipment, assistive technologies, and home modifications needed to live safely and independently, rather than needing to "save up" package funds for their purchases'.[1]

'INTERIM' HOME CARE PACKAGES

When a person is approved for a Home Care Package by the ACAT, the person has the option to accept or decline an 'interim' Home Care Package at the time of assessment. An interim package is a lower level HCP than the one the person is approved to receive.

The ACAT assessor should discuss the option of an interim package with you or your older loved one during the assessment. The conversation should address that if you're being approved for an HCP 3 that there will be a longer wait potentially for this higher

---

1   Support at Home Program Overview, page 3, January 2022.

level of package and you can accept a lower level HCP while waiting for the HCP 3 to be offered. So, if you're approved to receive an HCP 3, you can either wait until the HCP 3 is assigned to you or you might consider accepting an HCP 1 or HCP 2 until the level 3 package becomes available.

Accepting a lower level package is right for some people, but may not be right for others. Accepting a lower level HCP will provide you with in-home services and support sooner. If you choose to wait for the higher level of package to be assigned, that's okay.

If you are offered a lower level HCP because you agreed to this option when you had your ACAT assessment and later decide you don't want to accept the lower level package, that's alright too. You won't 'lose your place in the queue' by declining a lower level package.

* * *

Home Care Packages provide older people living at home with *coordinated* care.

Commonwealth Home Support Programme services can be provided by any number of providers, depending on how many CHSP referral codes a person has been approved for – this is regarded as 'fragmented care'. Home Care Packages are managed by one provider, the intent being that service provision is coordinated. Home Care Packages provide older people with greater choice and flexibility with service provision and – as a person's needs increase – the ability to upgrade to a higher level package.

These Home Care Packages are available to eligible older people now, but in mid 2023 these packages will be merged into the new aged-care system, Support at Home. We'll discuss this in greater detail in part V.

For now though, Home Care Packages will still be assigned to people waiting in the national priority queue, and these people won't miss out on receiving the support they have already been approved for by the ACAT. People will still be approved to receive Home Care Packages as they enter the aged-care system until the new system is implemented.

Let's now take a look at how someone is assessed by the team who approves Home Care Packages, the ACAT.

CHAPTER 13

WHAT IS THE AGED CARE ASSESSMENT TEAM?

Home Care Packages are assessed for and approved by the Aged Care Assessment Team (ACAT), or in Victoria, the Aged Care Assessment Service (ACAS).

The ACAT is made up of teams of experienced clinicians who complete in-depth assessments, known as 'comprehensive assessments', of older people seeking approval for Home Care Packages or access to residential respite or permanent entry into an aged-care facility.

ACAT assessors are also able to approve for CHSP-funded services and support, so if you've bypassed the RAS assessor and your older loved one has been assessed by an ACAT assessor, the ACAT can approve your older loved one for CHSP-funded services while you're waiting for the Home Care Package to be assigned.

ACATs are funded under the Commonwealth's Aged Care Assessment Program but employed under state or territory health services. ACAT offices are located across Australia, mostly in cities, but they have outreach options for people who live in rural and remote locations.

In this time of Covid disruption, many ACATs across Australia are assessing people over the phone. It's not ideal, but it's better than having ongoing delays in being assessed due to social distancing and quarantine.

HOW DOES THE ASSESSMENT WORK?

ACAT assessors are all experienced clinicians and comprise nurses, physiotherapists, occupational therapists, psychologists and social workers. They also work closely with geriatricians linked to memory clinics.

There is no benefit or disadvantage to having one type of clinician assess an older person compared with a clinician from another discipline. The experience ACAT assessors bring to an assessment is holistic and broad, and reflects their expertise in the specialty area of older persons' care. ACAT assessors use the same assessment documents and tools when assessing people regardless of the clinical discipline of the designated assessor. For example, an ACAT assessor who is a nurse will complete the same type of assessment as an ACAT assessor who is a social worker or physiotherapist. Ideally an ACAT assessment would occur in the older person's home, however there are circumstances and programs where an in-hospital assessment is appropriate.

For community-dwelling older people who wish to remain living in their own homes, the ACAT assessor would be assessing for a Home Care Package or Short-Term Restorative Care package and perhaps some CHSP services. For older people who would consider accessing respite in an aged-care facility or eventually move into an aged-care facility, the ACAT assessor would assess for access to this type of care at the same time they are assessing for a Home Care Package, if the person consents to having this done at the same time.

In my experience, being assessed for entry into an aged-care facility frightens some people as they think it means someone is going to 'ship them off' to a nursing home. It doesn't. A person cannot be entered into an aged-care facility without their consent, except in exceptional cases where an older person has impaired decision-making capacity and is at a high risk of adverse outcomes if they stay at home. In this instance, the legally appointed substitute decision maker would provide the consent on the older person's behalf.

Approval for Home Care Packages, residential respite and residential entry do not expire. The approval for these programs also carries across the country – being a federal program, the approval is recognised in any state or territory.

ACAT assessments ideally occur in the older person's home. The home environment can reveal a lot more information to an ACAT assessor than the older person will disclose over the phone.

Upon entry into an older person's home, the ACAT assessor is beginning to assess the older person by observation:

- Is the older person answering the door dishevelled or neatly dressed?
- Is there an odour emanating from the older person?
- Does the older person look underweight or malnourished?
- Do they have bruises or skin tears on their arms or legs?
- Have they admitted to just having gotten out of bed and it's 11am?
- Is the home cluttered or neat and tidy?
- Are there unopened medication boxes or Webster packs?

- Are the dishes unwashed and piled up in the kitchen?
- Is there an odour of spoiling food?
- Is there an odour of urine?

These observations are already forming a picture in the mind of the ACAT assessor before any conversations occur that will inform the assessment outcome.

Over the next one to two hours, the ACAT assessor will ask many questions to gather an in-depth appraisal of the older person's ability to manage at home, what their functional limitations are, and exactly how much support is required to allow the older person to remain living in their home. A family member or carer is welcome to participate in the ACAT assessment and provide information that the older person may forget to highlight.

Before the assessment can start, the ACAT assessor will confirm consent from the older person, ensuring they are willing to undergo the assessment. If the older person declines the assessment, it cannot proceed. This is another reason why having someone with the older person is worthwhile, particularly if the older person is suspicious and afraid or is cognitively impaired.

Reassuring the older person that the ACAT assessment will allow for in-home support to enable them to remain at home is important. I've had many older people initially decline an ACAT assessment because they thought the assessor was going to 'put me in a nursing home'.

There will be questions relating to what the older person's occupation was, what hobbies and pastimes the older person likes, their family network, who they regard as their support network (neighbours or friends) and questions about substitute decision makers and advance care planning.

The questions will then become more focused on functional ability; that is, the limitations the older person may have with completing their day-to-day activities, including any decline in mobility and their psychosocial wellbeing, including any memory deficits.

The questions that are asked as the assessment progresses through appraisal of function would include asking about:

- transferring in and out of bed or chairs, or getting up from the toilet
- distance that can be walked with or without a mobility aid
- any falls
- ability to complete household chores, including cleaning, laundry and garden maintenance
- meal preparation and appetite, and any difficulties swallowing
- weight loss
- personal care, including ability to shower safely unaided
- continence
- transport – their ability to drive, or if they rely on family or take public transport
- paying bills and financial management
- making appointments, and remembering to attend those appointments
- safety in the home.

Psychosocial appraisal of the older person would include questions relating to mood and memory loss. Specifically, an ACAT assessor will be asking the older person if they:

- enjoy doing the things they previously liked to do or have they given up those things

- keep in contact with friends or participate in community groups
- are eating well or are losing weight
- are struggling to get out of bed each day, preferring to sleep a lot
- call the family often during the day requiring reminders
- remember to take medication
- remember to attend appointments
- are unable to participate in a fluid conversation
- repeat previous discussions
- forget where they put things
- forget the names of friends or places they visited
- are getting lost at the shops or forgetting where they parked the car
- have had any minor traffic incidents.

The ACAT assessor will also explore health conditions and ask to see a list of medications. They may contact the GP to seek this information.

Carer dependency and associated carer stress is also explored during an ACAT assessment. A trigger for more urgent access to services or support is the ability of the carer to continue to support the older person.

Risk of carer crisis – that is, a carer who is so exhausted that they are thinking they cannot continue to care for their loved one – is a red flag to ACAT assessors and cause for more highly prioritised support to allow the carer to maintain their caring role and keep the older person in their own home, rather than prematurely entering an aged-care facility or hospital.

PREPARING FOR THE ASSESSMENT

Preparing thoroughly for an ACAT assessment is key to achieving the best outcome, which is approvals that will provide the right level of in-home support.

Many older people are reticent to acknowledge and receive services and support from people outside their family network. Many older people are very stoic and unwilling to admit they are struggling to manage and may need help. They often lack insight into the amount of support their family is providing, happily thinking their family is not inconvenienced, and will decline any external support for this reason.

Failing to recognise the level of support the family is providing and conveying that everything is okay will disadvantage the older person during an ACAT assessment. An older person who is steadfastly stoic and only wants family to support them will fail to receive approvals from the ACAT that accurately reflect the amount of support needed.

And an older person conveying they will wait until they *really* need the help will realise it is too late by the time they come around to accepting the assistance they need. There are many people waiting for ACAT assessments and tens of thousands of people waiting to receive services. Support doesn't happen instantly; it takes some time.

It is advisable to have a family member or carer with the older person when they are being assessed by the ACAT. The combined information that is imparted will ensure the ACAT assessor has a very clear picture of what is really going on within the older person's home. If it isn't possible to have a support person present with the older person, the assessor can speak with a family member or carer at another time.

* * *

ACAT clinicians are very good at what they do: assessing older people thoroughly. The knowledge and experience they have allows them to uncover information that would otherwise not seem significant to an older person or their family or carer.

An ACAT assessment is your loved one's opportunity to be approved for a Home Care Package at the right level, one that reflects their actual needs. Getting the right approvals depends on your preparedness for this assessment and willingness to be completely honest with the assessor.

Being approved for a Home Care Package is important to gain access to the national queue, because your older loved one will be waiting some months to be assigned a Home Care Package.

The ACAT assessor may also approve for another program – Short-Term Restorative Care – during the assessment, an excellent program that aims to re-able people and enhance their functional ability as much as possible while awaiting a Home Care Package.

Let's take a look now at Short-Term Restorative Care.

CHAPTER 14

WHAT IS SHORT-TERM RESTORATIVE CARE?

Being assessed by the ACAT provides access to a wider range of programs to support people living at home. A lesser known program, the Short-Term Restorative Care (STRC) program, is the most recent aged-care program subsidised by the government. The funding for this innovative program was announced in the 2015–16 Budget and successful ACAR applicants were assigned funding to deliver this program. The STRC program began rolling out via these successful providers in 2017.

In my opinion, it is the best program available to older people who are still living at home.

STRC comes under the flexible care funded programs. The funding for STRC is assigned to a provider, like CHSP. Only the providers who were successful in the ACARs are able to deliver this program.

This means that not all regions across the country are able to offer STRC. If there is no provider with STRC funding in a local area, it makes it very difficult – if not impossible – for people living in that location to access this program.

HOW DOES THE ASSESSMENT WORK?

STRC is aimed at reversing and/or slowing functional decline in older people, adopting a clinically led approach by engaging a team of clinicians to support the older person in regaining their wellbeing.[1]

STRC is delivered over eight weeks or 56 days. The program goes quickly and can seem to be a very busy time for people receiving STRC, as they may have multiple clinicians assessing and supporting them in this period.

One of the things I love about STRC is that nearly anyone could be considered eligible for the program. If an older person is experiencing a functional decline, if their mobility is becoming impaired, if they have lost the strength to complete their activities of daily living and they want to restore their wellbeing and continue to remain independent, STRC could be the program to support them to do this.

STRC is assessed by ACAT clinicians only. You will not be approved for STRC from a RAS assessment. If you feel this might be a program that you'd like access to, don't hesitate to mention this to the RAS assessor as they usually have very limited knowledge of this program.

---

1   www.health.gov.au/sites/default/files/documents/2020/12/short-term-restorative-care-programme-manual_0.pdf.

Being assessed for STRC

I've had many clients whose needs have increased since their most recent RAS assessment. They contact me to support them to get an ACAT assessment, hoping to be approved for a Home Care Package. In assessing these clients, I often realise they are eligible for STRC.

Having been previously assessed by RAS assessors, a new My Aged Care referral or support plan review will be directed to the RAS, as this is the last assessment team to have seen the older person. This is how the system works.

I know the older person is eligible for STRC and I go to great lengths in both my report and in the My Aged Care referral to detail this, as I'm hoping the RAS assessor will 'release' the referral and forward it onto the ACAT.

It is infrequent that the RAS assessor understands this process as nearly all RAS assessors I have dealt with are unaware of the STRC program. In fact, I have also had many conversations with the call centre staff at My Aged Care, telling them about this program and why my referral needs to be forwarded to the ACAT.

Mostly RAS assessors will call me and discuss my referral and agree to forward it to the ACAT. Sometimes they don't call and don't let my client know they aren't forwarding the referral to the ACAT. Why? Because they don't know what STRC is.

I follow up with my client and get to the bottom of it, then I call the RAS assessor and have a conversation, which turns into an education session about STRC. The RAS assessor then releases the referral straight away and allows the ACAT to accept it.

Being a clinically led program, the daily subsidy for STRC is paid at a higher rate than an HCP 4. The daily subsidy at the time of writing is $214.39, which equates to just over $12,000 over the 56 days.

Just like all the other programs available, this funding is not paid to your loved one. The funding sits with a provider and is allocated to your loved one when the provider offers you the STRC program.

It's excellent funding and can potentially include support from three different clinicians or more during this time; it really depends on what your loved one would like to receive and how often, over the eight-week program. The funding can also be used to purchase 'big ticket' items such as electric recliner chairs, mobility scooters, electric beds, and a wide range of equipment or modifications to enhance a person's wellbeing and independence.

I managed STRC for a provider for three years. I loved the program because the results some clients gained were nothing short of amazing.

A word of advice. While the ACAT assessors assess and approve for STRC, they don't always know what is possible from the program. Delivering the STRC program sits within a provider's role. So while the ACAT assessors have a good understanding of the program, the actual delivery of personalised support is determined by the provider, in consultation with the client, who needs to articulate the goals they want to achieve when they receive STRC.

What do you need to demonstrate to the ACAT assessors for them to approve your older loved one for STRC? You need to demonstrate limitations or impairment with their ability to complete activities of daily living independently, and they need to accept clinical support to help restore their independence.

Specifically, the ACAT will be looking at:

- impaired mobility that could be enhanced by receiving an eight-week in-home exercise program with an exercise physiologist or attending a physiotherapist clinic to regain strength and balance
- impaired mobility and difficulty completing tasks safely that could be supported by an occupational therapist assessment for prescription of mobility aids, equipment or modifications to the home to enhance safety
- pain, that could benefit from specialised physiotherapy or massage
- incontinence that could be assessed by a continence adviser and a prescription for continence aids
- podiatry, for assessment of gait and recommendation of orthotic inserts or shoes to improve stability with walking
- dietician for advice on diet, whether weight reduction or dietary sensitivities
- speech pathology if the older person has difficulty swallowing or speaking
- nursing, for wound care, stoma care or management of continence
- psychology for people experiencing grief, trauma or mental health issues.

Each person's STRC program is personalised according to their needs and goals.

The ACAT will develop a guiding plan, making recommendations for a provider to consider what the person may benefit from during STRC, but by the time the provider is able to deliver the program to the older person, their needs may have changed and they may have a different focus for regaining their independence.

An ACAT approval for STRC is valid for six months. For this reason, providers who deliver STRC will aim to get people onto the program as quickly as they can.

A person can be approved to receive two STRC programs in a 12-month period, but the ACAT cannot approve for both programs under the one approval. Given the intent is to restore a person's wellbeing to a point of potentially not needing further support, the person needs to complete their first STRC program, then the provider will review their goals at discharge from the program and if any goals remain unmet, the provider can refer back to the ACAT for consideration of a second round of STRC.

A person is able to receive CHSP-funded services while also receiving STRC. A person cannot receive a Home Care Package at the same time as STRC though, and people who live permanently in an aged-care facility are excluded from STRC.

STRC is ideally delivered in a person's home. The STRC programs I managed focused on bringing the clinicians to the home of the older person, so the client didn't have to drive, negotiating traffic and finding parking. It's not always possible to bring all clinicians to the home of the older person though, and this will depend on the model delivered by the provider in different locations across the country.

* * *

STRC will be merged into the new Support at Home Program mid 2023.

At the time of writing, the only sure thing we know is that whatever the new service will be that replaces STRC, it will be a 12-week timeframe rather than eight weeks as it is now.

There are many important learnings I want you to take away from reading this book. Knowing about STRC and how to go about being approved for it is up there in my top three things I really want you to know about.

The results I have seen in just eight weeks with many clients I've supported under this program have been remarkable. It's a fantastic program to get a lot sorted in a short timeframe, thereby potentially delaying the need for other support as a priority.

If your older loved one hasn't yet registered with My Aged Care or they are receiving only CHSP services, this is the opportunity to reflect on their functional ability, to determine if they would benefit from receiving coordinated support from a nurse, physiotherapist, exercise physiologist, occupational therapist or any other clinician, and to pursue a referral to the ACAT for STRC.

CHAPTER 15

WHAT IS THE TRANSITION CARE PROGRAM?

The Transition Care Program (TCP) also falls under the flexible care model and provides short-term support to assist an older person to 'get back on their feet' after a hospital admission.

Similar to STRC, the orientation with TCP is having a team of clinicians support a person who is in hospital to transition home safely and regain their strength and wellbeing at home. The difference between TCP and STCR is that eligibility for TCP is a hospital admission whereas eligibility for STRC is functional decline in the community without a recent hospital admission.

HOW DOES THE ASSESSMENT WORK?

The person must have been reasonably independent and managing well before coming into hospital, but the acute illness or injury has caused some functional decline or limitations in the person's ability to manage as well as they did before being admitted to hospital. A person must be in hospital when the referral for TCP occurs.

Presentations at an emergency department or a brief admission to hospital will not support a TCP referral though, as the process of assessing someone and getting them onto the program takes some time.

People cannot go home and then be referred for TCP. The TCP team must receive the referral while the older person is in hospital, assess them while they are in hospital, and then accept them onto the program and facilitate their discharge home from hospital to begin TCP.

Any clinician on the person's hospital treating team can make a referral to TCP. Often it will be a physiotherapist or occupational therapist (OT), as these are two of the main clinicians who work in the TCP team. The hospital physiotherapist will speak with the TCP physiotherapist and the hospital OT will speak with the TCP OT, and between the hospital treating team and the TCP team they'll determine if a person can be accepted onto the program at discharge. Because TCP is a clinician-led program, the referrals between the hospital and the TCP team generally occur from one clinician to another, but it may also be a junior doctor referring to the TCP admin person or the ward social worker referring to TCP admin.

It doesn't really matter who makes the referral, as long as it is done in plenty of time for the TCP team to review it and see if they have capacity to accept a person onto the program without delay.

A referral to the TCP team should not occur as someone is about to be discharged from hospital – a week before would be the bare minimum. Any less than one week does not give the TCP team time to act on the referral. The treating medical team will already be planning for your loved one's discharge.

With hospital beds always full and management expecting the medical team to have people discharged as quickly as possible to free up beds for people coming in via the emergency department, the treating team will aim to discharge a person on the proposed date; they won't want to wait for another week until the TCP team has processed the referral and comes to the hospital to complete their assessment.

My advice to my clients is to begin asking about or suggesting TCP to your older loved one's treating team as soon as possible after admission to hospital. TCP is a program that's in high demand. There is always a waitlist. When people are assessed in hospital to be discharged home on TCP, they must stay in hospital until a place on TCP becomes available. This is another reason why a referral to TCP needs to occur as soon as possible.

There is so much pressure on medical teams to discharge people and free up beds that this will unfortunately prevent some people getting access to excellent programs such as TCP. I've been involved with clients who were perfectly suited to going home on TCP, but the treating medical team refused to allow the referral because it would delay the discharge.

Older people in both public and private hospitals are eligible to be considered for TCP. Being a private patient in a private hospital does not exclude your older loved one from being considered for this program.

HOW DOES TCP WORK?

The duration of TCP is up to 12 weeks. Some older people need the entire 12 weeks to regain their optimal functioning and some people need less time. The amount of time a TCP episode runs for will be determined by the TCP clinicians in consultation with yourself and your older loved one. It is also possible to get an extension to the TCP episode of up to 42 days. This extension is determined by your older loved one's treating TCP team during the time they are receiving this program.

TCP can be delivered in a variety of settings, with the aim to have your older loved one complete their program at home. An older person could also be discharged to their son's or daughter's home for a short time and then move back to their own home, all the while being on TCP.

TCP can be delivered in a residential aged-care setting too; that is, beds in an aged-care facility are arranged as part of the program and therapy can be delivered in this setting to start off with, aiming to support your older loved one to move back home while still receiving TCP. This does not mean a person is being admitted to the facility permanently.

TCP is aimed at preventing older people from having to move into an aged-care facility prematurely. If your plan is to move your older loved one into an aged-care facility after leaving hospital, they would be ineligible for TCP. Remember, the goal of TCP is to get your older loved one back on their feet so they can remain at home.

Another excellent aspect of this program is that if your older loved one is already receiving a Home Care Package, they are still eligible to receive TCP. The HCP will need to be 'paused' while your older loved one is on TCP, and at the conclusion of their TCP episode, they revert to receiving the HCP.

A successful use of TCP

My dad had an HCP 4.

He had four strokes in the last year of his life, each time being admitted to hospital. For two of these hospital admissions, including the last admission, we had Dad discharged home on TCP. Dad was not going to be admitted to an aged-care facility and the previous time he was discharged home from hospital on TCP he did really well, regaining his function.

Dad's HCP funding had hit its limit; there was no funding left to engage a physio or an OT at home. And 'saving up' enough funding to have a physio or OT come to Dad's home would take many months. Getting Dad home and keeping him at home was possible only with TCP.

Dad required two people to help him transfer when he first came home after that fourth stroke. He had some strength in his legs, but he couldn't get out of a chair or bed by himself. It was very heavy work in those first couple of weeks home after the fourth stroke.

But gradually he became stronger. He did the exercises with his carer every day, and by the end of the 12 weeks was getting out of a chair and out of bed by himself and was able to walk without a mobility aid.

After that fourth stroke, Dad remained at home until January the following year, when he left us.

Without TCP to support Dad to come home after that fourth stroke, I don't know how we would have managed this.

When the TCP team receive your older loved one's referral from the hospital treating team, they will liaise with the hospital team to ascertain how close your older loved one is to being discharged. They'll be watching how they progress in recovery from illness or injury, and when the hospital team decides your older loved one is almost ready to go home, the hospital team and TCP team will decide upon a discharge date together.

The TCP team will then begin planning your older loved one's supported transition home. Specifically, the TCP physio will be talking with the hospital physio about continuity of a prescribed physio program, the occupational therapists from both the hospital and TCP will be discussing what equipment or modifications may be necessary to support functional optimisation at home, and the nurses may be discussing ongoing wound care.

If your older loved one needs some assistance with showering, this can also be arranged, as can assistance with cleaning the house, shopping and meal preparation. All these services will be arranged via the TCP team.

In the first couple of weeks after being discharged from hospital, your older loved one will be visited at the location they are receiving TCP by all the clinicians involved in their care. As the program progresses and your older loved one improves, the clinicians will hand over to their allied health assistants.

The physio will prescribe an exercise program and an assistant may visit thereafter to supervise progress. It will be expected that your older loved one will attend to their exercises each day so they can show the therapist progress over time. The occupational therapist will have hired equipment such as shower chairs and mobility equipment and arranged to have grab rails or ramps installed as required.

Nurses will continue to provide wound care or specialised clinical support if required.

If your older loved one was receiving services and support from CHSP prior to the hospital admission, these services can continue as long as they aren't the same as services TCP is providing. For example, if your older loved one received cleaning under CHSP funding prior to the hospital admission, TCP won't also provide cleaning.

* * *

TCP is an excellent program to support a discharge home from hospital. It's designed to get your older loved one back on their feet, literally. Like STRC, it's a program I want everyone to know about, because no one can anticipate a hospital admission and if your older loved one is in hospital and going to need support at home on discharge then this could be the program.

Don't delay in asking your older loved one's hospital treating team about TCP if your loved one is admitted to hospital. The sooner you highlight this as an option, the better the chance of having the treating team support this plan for discharge.

PART IV

WHAT ELSE DO YOU NEED TO KNOW?

CHAPTER 16

WHAT HAPPENS AFTER AN ASSESSMENT?

Understanding what happens after your older loved one has had an assessment is important. If you understand what happens next, you're in the best position to follow through on any approvals your older loved one has received and ensure those approved services commence as intended.

If your older loved one has had a RAS assessment, it's essential you ask them what services they are going to approve and who they are going to forward those approvals to. Remember, if the RAS assessor forwards their approvals to CHSP providers and the CHSP providers don't have capacity to deliver those services, you'll be waiting for a phone call that isn't going to happen. Your older loved one will not receive that approved service and you won't know unless you follow up with the provider.

HOW LONG DOES IT TAKE?

Your older loved one will eventually receive a letter and documents stating what services have been approved with the corresponding referral codes. In my experience this takes some weeks to occur. The quickest I have known of clients receiving these approval documents is two weeks, and most of my clients tell me it takes three to four weeks before they receive the letter and documentation in the post.

Hold on to these documents; you'll need them down the track. If you haven't already created a file to keep all your loved one's aged-care correspondence in, now is the time to sort it.

The same process occurs after an ACAT assessment. The ACAT assessor will give you a good idea during the assessment what they are going to approve for, but their assessment has to be reviewed by a delegate – who is another clinician in the team – and approved by them.

Sometimes a delegate might disagree with the assessor, so although the assessor has indicated to you what they are going to approve for, it may not be approved by the delegate. In my experience, it is not the level of package that is disputed between the ACAT assessor and delegate but the priority, being the urgency with which the ACAT are recommending the person be assigned the package.

ACATs approve for STRC and HCPs according to how urgently a person needs services. The approval might be low, medium or high priority. These priority levels reflect how long a person will wait for services. Having the Home Care Package approved as a high priority means this approval will move to the front of the national queue and the person won't wait as long for their package to be assigned. The great majority of approvals happen as a medium priority. A lesser number of HCP approvals are given a high priority, and I haven't ever seen a low-priority approval.

With STRC and the approval only lasting for six months, once the provider receives the approval they will be actioning that as quickly as they can and the STRC program will be offered within six months.

Previously a medium priority was recognised as being 12 to 18 months wait and a high priority about nine months. Towards the end of 2021 and through 2022 the Federal Government has injected more funding into the Home Care Package program to create more packages, and we are seeing people who have been approved at a medium priority receive assignment of their package in 3 to 6 months and a high-priority package be assigned in 1 to 3 months.

But it also depends on how long your older loved one has already been waiting in the queue to have their Home Care Package assigned, and also at what level the HCP is approved at. The lower level packages, the HCP 1s and 2s, are assigned sooner as there are more of those levels of packages available, and HCP 3s and 4s take longer to be assigned because there are fewer of those HCPs being subsidised.

I had a client who 'got lost in the system'. They had received an approval for an HCP 2 two years previously, but didn't recall receiving any documentation about the approval. In this case the assignment of the HCP would have lapsed as the client did not accept the HCP within the timeframe of 56 days, due to not knowing about the package being assigned.

When the client contacted me and then contacted My Aged Care to discuss this situation, the HCP 2 was assigned immediately because that lapsed time was regarded as 'still waiting in the queue'.

If your older loved one is approved for STRC, the ACAT will often forward the approval to one of the few local STRC providers in your area or they may leave it in the My Aged Care portal for a provider to accept. I have experienced both, but more often than not the ACAT will call a provider and discuss a client's needs and determine if the provider can deliver the services the client is needing. Therefore, you or your older loved one are likely to be contacted by the STCR provider and informed the approval has been accepted. You'll then discuss with the provider arranging a date for them to 'onboard' your older loved one to their service to receive STRC.

If your older loved one has been approved for a Home Care Package, the approval will join the waitlist for a package to become available. As HCPs become available, your older loved one's approval will move to the front of the queue.

Previously, the number of people waiting in the queue to be assigned a Home Care Package was 100,000, and at times this was even higher. With the injection of funding towards the end of 2021, the number of people waiting to be assigned their approved level of Home Care Package at September 2021 was 74,000.[1]

The government has committed to funding 80,000 new Home Care Packages at a cost of $6.5 billion, with 40,000 of these new HCPs being released during 2021–22 and the remaining 40,000 to be released in the latter half of 2022–23.

---

1   www.gen-agedcaredata.gov.au/www_aihwgen/media/Home_care_report/Home-Care-Data-Report-1st-Qtr-2021-22.pdf.

MANAGING THE DOCUMENTATION

After the ACAT has approved your older loved one for an HCP and the approval has entered the queue, you can call My Aged Care and ask them to tell you how long it might be before the HCP is assigned. My Aged Care cannot give exact dates, but they'll let you know if it is maybe six months or three months.

The next letter you or your older loved one will receive will be about three months before the HCP is due to be assigned. At this time consideration should be given to the model of HCP management your older loved one might favour, being fully managed or self-managed. Or you might choose to part manage the HCP, having some help from a provider but still arranging some aspects of service provision yourself.

The final letter your older loved one will receive is advising the HCP is assigned. This letter will advise your older loved one they have 56 days to accept and sign up with a provider. The HCP will be revoked if they haven't signed with a provider in 56 days.

These ACAT approvals and the letters that follow confuse people.

I've had many conversations with people who think that the approval letter from the ACAT is the offer of an HCP. It's not. There are three letters and accompanying documents that will arrive in the post. It's the final letter advising assignment of the HCP that is the one to get excited about.

* * *

Understanding what happens after a RAS or ACAT assessment is as important as being prepared for these assessments in the first place. The system is not failsafe. People still get lost in the system.

People don't understand that ignoring the letter advising the Home Care Package is assigned leads to urgency weeks down the track when you need to have made that decision about who you're going to choose to provide your older loved one's package. The only people who are going to call about the assignment of a Home Care Package are the providers who can see the approval in the My Aged Care portal. They'll see your older loved one has been assigned a Home Care Package before you're advised.

These providers might have been acceptable to provide your CHSP services, but if you're seeking greater choice or want to self-manage your Home Care Package, you're the one who has to take a proactive approach and contact your preferred provider.

CHAPTER 17

HOW DO WE CHOOSE A PROVIDER FOR A HOME CARE PACKAGE?

Choosing a provider for your older loved one's Home Care Package can be one of the most confusing and challenging aspects of accepting services and support. There are so many providers; how do you work out which provider is right for your older loved one? Should they stay with the provider who has been providing CHSP-funded services because your older loved ones knows the support staff? Does your older loved one want to sign up with a faith-based organisation based on their religious beliefs? Are you attracted to a provider who says they don't charge fees? Will you engage a broker – a company that advertises that they will find a provider for you?

Home Care Packages are revenue for providers and the market-place is competitive for your dollar; that is, your funding.

Choice and flexibility underpin the way services and support are delivered for people with Home Care Packages, whether your provider offers a fully managed model or self-management.

Fully managed Home Care Package providers, also known as 'traditional' providers, comprise the majority of organisations administering Home Care Package funding on behalf of people receiving an HCP. Fully managed providers can be faith-based organisations, not-for-profit organisations or they can be private companies.

Organisations that support you to self-manage your Home Care Package are less common but are certainly gaining attention and popularity with older people who have the ability to source and manage their own support.

The companies that have emerged as the leading providers of self-managed Home Care Packages are private organisations. We discuss the pros and cons of fully managed and self-managed options in the next chapter. Right now I'll just let you know how I advise my clients on how to choose a provider that is right for their needs.

CHOOSING A PROVIDER THAT IS RIGHT FOR YOUR OLDER LOVED ONE

So, you've received the letter that informs you that your older loved one has been assigned a Home Care Package.

When you receive the letter of assignment of a Home Care Package you have 56 days to sign up with a provider. It is possible to ask for an extension if your circumstances have prevented you from choosing a provider in this timeframe. An extension of 28 days is possible. Contact My Aged Care to discuss extending the acceptance date if you find yourself in this predicament.

Choosing a Home Care Package provider for your older loved one's Home Care Package requires careful consideration. What works well for one person may not work well for another.

Fees

How providers administer Home Care Packages differs greatly, with different fee structures and costs. They even have different names for their fees. This is the cause of most confusion for a person trying to decide which provider to sign with. The different names providers use for the fees they charge include:

- administration fees
- case management fees
- package management fees
- care coordination fees.

Providers will deduct anywhere from 10% to 50% of your subsidy for their fees. Fully managed providers generally deduct 25% to 35% of your subsidy.

Providers may also charge your package for processing invoices from subcontractors too, adding an additional 10% of the total invoice to cover the time it takes them to process these invoices. Some providers will charge the Basic Daily Fee, and many won't.

And then there are providers who advertise they don't charge any fees.

The My Aged Care website has a 'Find a Provider' option where people are able to search by location and postcode to see what providers service their local area. It's not entirely accurate and some providers listed don't service some local areas though they advertise they do.

This 'Find a Provider' option also allows people to compare providers.

Comparing providers on the My Aged Care website won't give you much clarity about which provider to choose; the comparison tables just don't give enough detailed information to make an informed choice. Start there, but do the legwork, make the phone calls and meet providers face to face to elicit the details you need to make your choice.

Making a decision on which provider to use should not be based solely on fees. The decision should also consider continuity of staff, effective and timely communication, and the provider being willing to consider your loved one's personal needs.

Choosing a Home Care Package provider should also consider how much control, flexibility and choice you desire. It should consider your ability to source all your services and support yourself and manage your monthly subsidy or leave this for someone else to manage. Self-managing a Home Care Package is right for some people and signing with a fully managed provider is right for other people. There is also the option to go with a part-managed provider too.

Most people I interact with, my clients and people I am engaging with on social media or in my community, have a good idea if they could self-manage or not, and understanding this guides them as to which providers to seek out and compare.

In my experience, it's the people who want to sign up with a fully managed provider who struggle with making a decision about choosing the provider that best meets their needs and understanding what will be charged to deliver their services.

So, how does one make this decision?

Availability of services

You start with a wishlist.

The only way to compare apples with apples is to write down what you think your older loved one needs most from the package subsidy. What services or support are most important to meeting the older person's needs and supporting them at home?

Services to consider include:

- someone to clean the home each week
- someone to mow the yard
- supply of meals
- someone to clean the heating and air conditioner systems
- a nurse, OT or physio.

Also consider the distance the support workers need to travel to come to your loved one's home as travel costs will be billed from the HCP funding.

Your wishlist needs to be detailed. I encourage people to write down as many things as they can that they might want to use their package subsidy for.

Then I encourage people to do some research, talking to people in their local community to see what they are saying about the providers in that location. People who are happy with their package provider will be telling everyone, just as those who are unhappy will be telling people.

When you, or your older loved one, has an idea who is more reputable in your location, contact three providers and ask to meet with them. At the meeting, show them your wishlist and ask them how many of these services could be covered by your subsidy.

This will give you an idea how far your subsidy will stretch based on the support you're wanting for your older loved one. The provider can't hide behind confusing language relating to fees; they'll have to cost what you want and let you know what's achievable and what's not from your wishlist.

The provider should also be taking into account the time taken for carers or support workers to travel to your home to deliver these services. Travel time and mileage may also be deducted from your package subsidy.

Continuity of staff

Another topic to discuss with potential providers is continuity of staff. Older people generally like to know who is coming to help them shower, clean their home or do their grocery shopping. Older people are reassured that their carer or support worker knows them and understands their preferences.

Continuity of staff is especially important for people with dementia. Familiarity with staff is as important for the older person as it is for the older person's family, who depend on the reassurance familiarity brings to personalised support for their older loved one.

If a provider tells you they don't provide continuity of staff because they believe it creates dependency or the professional relationship may become too close, this is likely to be their way of *not* saying that they don't have enough staff to provide the continuity. In my experience, the providers who won't commit to providing continuity of staff are the providers who cannot retain staff.

The decision about who is coming into the home of your older loved one is a significant one and your older loved one needs to trust their carers or support workers. Providers who do their best to roster the same staff to their clients tend to have a better relationship with their clients.

Remember, service provision is consumer directed. It's your decision if you want the same few carers or support workers tending to your loved one or if you don't mind having different carers every day; it's not for the provider to tell you how it is going to be.

* * *

Choosing a provider for your older loved one's Home Care Package is a big decision.

The decision is entirely yours and your older loved one's to make and should not be influenced by a CHSP provider telling you they are going to be taking over or continuing to deliver their support when the Home Care Package begins. The decision should also not be based solely on costs. It might sound attractive to sign with a provider who charges no fees or only 10% fees, but all providers have to make money to keep their businesses viable, regardless of whether they are not-for-profit or for-profit. If they say there are no fees you will be paying in some other way.

Choosing a provider for a Home Care Package is a personal decision and should be based on the individual needs of the older person. Your older loved one has 56 days to sign up with a package provider; take this time to do your homework so that you're comfortable that who you choose will work with you and your older loved one to deliver services that reflect their individual needs.

CHAPTER 18

WHAT'S THE DIFFERENCE BETWEEN FULLY MANAGED AND SELF-MANAGED?

Home Care Package providers have traditionally operated under a fully managed model until an alternative model, self-management, entered the market. Self-management is an attractive option and is gaining popularity as it gives people greater choice and flexibility with their in-home service provision.

Which model is right for your older loved one is a decision that requires research and a good understanding of the benefits and drawbacks of each model. Prior to receiving the letter notifying that your loved one has been assigned a Home Care Package, you will have hopefully been looking at different providers of Home Care Packages in your area.

Don't leave doing your research until you get that letter as you only have 56 days to decide on your preferred package provider. And 56 days goes quickly.

Talking to other people in the local area will give you insight into how different providers manage care provision within Home Care Packages. If your older loved one is part of community groups or support groups, ask other members if they have a Home Care Package and who provides their services and support. Ask older friends if they are happy with the provider of their package. Ask local allied health clinicians if they have heard who has a good reputation as a provider of Home Care Packages.

Some people will ask the ACAT assessor who they recommend. While ACAT assessors often have a good idea which providers are doing a good job of supporting their clients and are aware of the providers who people complain about, they are unlikely to tell you. The ACAT assessors are impartial and cannot recommend one provider over another. Home Care Packages are revenue for providers and your subsidy equals their income stream. Providers can be aggressive in pursuing people who have been assigned their Home Care Package, but it is solely your decision who you choose to sign up with to deliver your services.

FULLY MANAGED PACKAGES

Fully managed providers, as mentioned previously, typically charge or deduct around 25% to 35% of your subsidy to manage the package. What does this mean? Managing a Home Care Package means taking responsibility for all the government reporting required to demonstrate how the subsidy has been spent. The providers who offer a fully managed model have bricks-and-mortar offices and higher overheads that need to be paid for. The provider needs to cover the costs of keeping their business running, with the administration fee paying for any number of costs associated with their business, such as employing the admin staff, furnishing their offices, keeping a fleet of vehicles and running their software.

Fully managed providers however do everything for you. Sourcing and coordinating your services and support under a fully managed model is undertaken by the provider and this is also why you're paying around 30% in fees. They employ and supply your carers or support workers, provide subcontractors such as cleaners or lawn-mowing contractors, arrange for assessments from clinicians and ensure that your requests are acted upon as your needs change.

If your older loved one's carer or cleaner calls in sick, the provider will source a substitute carer or cleaner. If a subcontracted lawn-mowing company hasn't done a good job of mowing the lawn, the provider should take up your concern on your older loved one's behalf with the lawn-mowing company.

SELF-MANAGED PACKAGES

Self-managing a Home Care Package is an attractive option for people who are able to do this. Self-management is becoming a viable option for people who have the 'know how' and ability to source their own care workers. By sourcing carers or support workers and finding your own contractor to clean your loved one's home, mow the lawn or attend to home modifications, you're going to save money in admin fees.

Self-managed providers still need to charge an admin-type fee, as they too must maintain compliance and complete reporting for the government about subsidy expenditure, but the admin fees are significantly less. Providers of self-managed Home Care Packages typically charge between 10% and 17% to administer the funds provided by the government.

Compared to fully managed providers, these fees are significantly lower.

Sounds appealing, doesn't it? Lower admin fees are certainly a reason for considering signing up with a self-managed provider or moving to one if you're older loved one is already with a fully managed provider, but the fees alone should not be the determining factor.

Sourcing your own carers or support workers takes time and effort. Screening prospective carers, and chasing them to get their Covid vaccination certificates, police checks and business documentation takes time. If your carer is sick or going away on holidays, it's up to you to find an alternative carer. And the responsibility for managing expenditure rests with you too.

My experience with self-managed and fully managed providers

My dad had an HCP 4 and was with a fully managed provider. He had dementia and had four strokes in the last year of his life.

My parents live in the same town as I do and my youngest sister also lives locally. I was working full-time and raising kids during this last year of my dad's life. My husband is a FIFO worker. While my mum shouldered most of the care for Dad, my sister and I also supported Mum to support Dad.

I used to go around to my parents' home after work and take Dad for a drive many afternoons, as this was our strategy to manage his sundowning. It also gave Mum a couple of hours to herself or to prepare dinner.

After coming home from the drive, I would shower Dad if his carer had been unable to convince him to have a shower that day.

On weekends I used to shower Dad as the cost of having a carer on the weekends exceeded the amount of funding available.

Those months were a blur of trying to keep my head above water, meeting all the commitments of my own family, my job and supporting Mum and Dad. There was no way we could have self-managed Dad's HCP for him. The provider we had was excellent and responded to his changing needs efficiently. We were happy to pay the 30% admin fees and allow the provider to do all the work for us.

My mum was with a fully managed provider with her HCP 2, the same provider who had managed Dad's HCP. But the provider was taken over by a larger provider and the quality of service declined.

Mum wasn't reviewed since she signed up with the provider, her care plan was not updated as her needs changed and it felt like there was an expectation that I sort everything for Mum. In fact, I was. I was managing my mum's Home Care Package, but the provider was deducting 30% in fees.

Eventually I decided to move Mum to a self-managed provider. It was the best decision we made for Mum. The admin fees dropped from 30% to 10%, freeing up more of the subsidy for Mum to use for support.

The self-managed provider is outstanding. They took the time to understand Mum's needs and develop a care plan that is so detailed and personalised it allows for greater choice with how she wants to spend her funding.

The flexibility that this self-managed provider offers is also noteworthy.

Mum's needs are not as complex as Dad's were and my kids are now adults and have moved out of home, so the competing demands I had when caring for Dad have changed, freeing up some time so I can manage Mum's Home Care Package on her behalf.

People contact me to ask my advice about self-managing. The older people contact me, and adult children also contact me to discuss the pros and cons. We discuss their situation and determine if self-managing is going to be too time intensive or if they have the capacity to take this on.

It's vital people are aware of the limitations of self-managing. It's a fantastic option for people who can handle it but is an added stressor for people who are already time poor.

How do you self-manage? There are a handful of companies who provide the option for recipients of Home Care Packages to self-manage.

These companies are located in larger metropolitan cities and operate from a centralised head office. Self-managed providers do not have offices in local areas.

How this works as compared to a fully managed provider is that geography does not impact on the process of administering a self-managed package; that is, the management of the funding and reporting requirements can occur anywhere.

The recipient of the Home Care Package or their family member or carer liaise with the coordinator of the self-managed package via phone, as opposed to face to face with fully managed providers who typically have bricks-and-mortar offices. Having said this though, some self-managed providers are brokering to other companies in regional locations and using these other companies as a proxy representation for their organisation.

Once you've decided which self-managed company you want to sign up with, you enter into an agreement with them, the same as you would with a fully managed provider.

Then it's over to you to find your carers or support workers, contractors and clinicians.

* * *

Choosing to have your older loved one's Home Care Package managed by a fully managed or self-managed provider is a personalised decision. There are pros and cons with each model. Self-management is an attractive option but one with a significant commitment of time from you.

Be realistic about which model is right for your older loved one's situation. Base your decision on what is going to work well for both you and your family. Some people like to start with a fully managed provider and once they understand the system better, they feel confident to move to self-management. The marketplace is about choice. Which model you choose needs to reflect your circumstances.

CHAPTER 19

WHAT DO WE DO IF CARE NEEDS INCREASE?

Your older loved one has been assessed by the RAS or ACAT and your approvals have either been forwarded to a CHSP provider or to an STRC provider or entered the national priority queue to await assignment of a Home Care Package. Now you're waiting. Waiting to hear from a CHSP provider or an STRC provider or to have your Home Care Package assigned.

During this waiting time, things could change. They could change rapidly, or it could be a progressive decline of function over months.

Or perhaps you're receiving a Home Care Package but your older loved one's needs have increased. If your older loved one's needs have increased and the level of Home Care Package isn't enough to meet the increased needs, you need to go back to My Aged Care and request a support plan review.

TRIGGERING A NEW ASSESSMENT

You'll need to think about this conversation before contacting My Aged Care and have written down all the reasons why you're requesting a support plan review. You'll need to give My Aged Care as much detail as possible.

Triggering a support plan review within the system means that the last team to assess your older loved one will be the team to review and reassess. Either team can approve for some additional support, the RAS referring on to the ACAT or the ACAT upgrading the level of Home Care Package or the level of priority previously approved.

If the RAS were the previous assessor, it would be appropriate that they forward the referral to the ACAT. It is logical that over time an older person's needs increase as they become frailer, so referring on to the ACAT is ideal. I've spoken with RAS assessors though who are reluctant to refer on to the ACAT at a support plan review. A RAS assessor reviewing an older person and approving them for more CHSP-funded services when they aren't receiving any services because there is no capacity with local CHSP providers is not appropriate. Referring on to the ACAT for STRC or an HCP is the appropriate step to take in this situation.

If it was the ACAT who previously assessed your older loved one, they have a few options. Let's look at the different scenarios.

If you've been approved by the ACAT to receive a Home Care Package and you understand that package was approved at a medium priority, you can discuss with the ACAT assessor about upgrading the priority to a high priority. A high-priority approval will see your older loved one assigned a Home Care Package sooner.

If your older loved one is receiving a Home Care Package that isn't meeting their needs – that is, there isn't enough funding to provide the support required – again, you would be contacting My Aged Care about a support plan review and discussing with the ACAT about them reassessing your older loved one for a package upgrade to the next level.

The ACAT, being the top level of assessment team, can also approve for CHSP-funded services and support in addition to someone receiving a Home Care Package. This is known as a 'top up', and is a way of potentially accessing CHSP services to fill the gap in service provision until your older loved one is assigned a Home Care Package at the level now needed. These CHSP top up services will only be provided until the higher level of Home Care Package is assigned.

CARER CRISIS

Another trigger for a support plan review is carer crisis.

We acknowledge the significant amount of support informal carers provide to assist someone to stay at home. We also acknowledge that caring for someone with complex or high needs takes a toll. We call this 'carer stress'.

Because ACATs have become more constrained in approving people as high priority for their Home Care Packages, ACATs will discuss carer stress versus carer crisis to determine if they can approve someone as a high priority.

There isn't enough funding to allow every older person who needs a Home Care Package to be assigned one quickly. Remember, the priority rating relates to the time a person will wait in the queue to be assigned their Home Care Package. A medium priority approval is about a six- to nine-month wait and a high priority is about three to six months.

If every older person who needed a high-priority approval received one, there would be an increased demand in the queue for people to be assigned their Home Care Packages sooner. ACATs around the country have told me they are supposed to approve no more than approximately 13% of people as a high priority, though they know the percentage of people needing their Home Care Package within three months is much higher. One ACAT team leader told me they must be very careful with how many high-priority approvals they grant or 'the department will beat us with their big stick'.

So what's the difference between carer stress and carer crisis? To me, there is no difference but I'm sure some ACAT delegates would disagree with me. I've been a carer and I speak with carers every day. I see their exhaustion and the despair. I sense their guilt at not being able to go on. I've consoled them while they cry.

I have a document from My Aged Care titled 'ACAT Guidance for Home Care Package High Priority'. It defines carer crisis as being 'the carer is in crisis or no longer able to provide care due to: a change in the carer/s personal circumstances ie death/significant decline in carer's own health status or an inability to sustain their caring role due to a lack of assistance being received.'[1]

This document goes on to describe that a carer in crisis is different to caregiver stress. Caregiver stress is a condition of exhaustion, anger or guilt that results from unrelieved caring for a chronically ill dependent. The stress can vary depending on the individual, and generally does not prohibit the carer from providing care. Caregiver stress can be reduced by accessing respite care.

---

1   agedcare.royalcommission.gov.au/system/files/202006/RCD.9999.0140.0001.pdf.

Let's be honest – that's splitting hairs.

A carer who is exhausted and angry is not far from being in crisis.

Putting my nurse hat back on for a moment, when I still worked in the hospital, I'd see carers present at the emergency department with symptoms of a stroke. These carers would not be able to speak, or one side of their body had become paralysed. I've also seen carers present with seizures. But these presentations weren't strokes or epilepsy, it was conversion disorder. These carers were exhausted and angry, but they kept soldiering on, and their bodies shut down on them due to the incredible amount of stress they were experiencing.

I once had an ACAT assessor tell me she wouldn't approve for a higher level of Home Care Package because the older lady had an approval for residential respite, and if her daughter really wanted a break she should put her in a nursing home for a couple of weeks. The old lady had dementia, anxiety, and was vision impaired. Separating her from her daughter would have been traumatic for both the older lady and her daughter. This response from this ACAT assessor was inappropriate and cruel.

What do I tell carers who feel they can't go on?

I suggest they wait until a day when they feel stronger and pick that day to contact My Aged Care and be assertive and not take no for an answer. Or to have a family member, friend or neighbour sit with them while they make the call, to provide support.

Often these carers tell me they just don't have the energy to do anything else. If you're feeling like this now, it's not unusual. Find someone to talk to, write a list of all the reasons you think you can't continue to support your older loved one, and contact My Aged Care on a day you're feeling a little stronger. It's important you dig a little deeper and seek the increased support your older loved one needs.

OTHER AGED-CARE PROGRAMS THAT MIGHT HELP

What else is available to older people who are waiting for their Home Care Package to be assigned or to be upgraded to the next level of package?

There are other federally funded schemes outside the aged-care system and there are a number of state- and territory-funded programs or schemes as well. The intent of these state-funded programs is similar, but between the states and territories the names of the programs and schemes differ. It's impossible to list all of these here, but I'll steer you in the direction to potentially access additional services or funding:

- Carer Gateway is a federally funded service providing phone, online or face-to-face support for carers.

- Carer's allowance or payments can be accessed via Services Australia and is an allowance or 'pension' for people who are providing support for a family member. There are of course eligibility criteria for both the allowance and the payment.

- Continence Aids Payment Scheme is a federally funded program to assist people with an allocation of funding to purchase continence products.

- The state and territory health departments also offer access to programs that supply people with continence aids, mobility aids, oxygen equipment and other assistive technology. All these state- and territory-funded programs have different names, but a quick Google search will connect you with your state health department site and detail how you access these programs.

- Medicare also subsidises access to allied health clinicians on referral from a GP. This support is known as either a GP Management Plan or a Team Care Arrangement.

- Some local councils offer a service whereby on garbage day, the garbage collector will go into the older person's yard, collect their bin, empty it and return it, so the older person doesn't have to risk a fall putting their garbage bin out and taking it in. Call your older loved one's local council to find out if they offer this; it's easy to arrange and is at no additional cost to the older person.

- There are many support groups in local areas that are run by volunteers. Aside from offering social connection and support, these groups are also proactive in finding out what services and support are available locally.

* * *

If your older loved one's care needs increase after they've been approved for CHSP services or approved by the ACAT for a Home Care Package, it's important to speak up. They don't have to wait in the queue, struggling to get by until the support becomes available. It's important to take action to receive the support sooner.

Being reviewed by the ACAT and reclassified as a high priority instead of a medium priority will shorten the wait time until your older loved one's Home Care Package is assigned by many months.

The system isn't intuitive, and RAS and ACAT assessors won't know your older loved one's need for in-home support has become a matter of urgency until you take action. Understanding how the priority system works, recognising increasing frailty and dependence on family for support, and adopting a proactive approach to enabling the support to be delivered as a matter of urgency will ensure your older loved one is able to stay at home, supported by the aged-care programs that are designed to keep them there.

PART V

THE 2023 AGED-CARE REFORMS AND WHAT THEY MEAN FOR YOU

CHAPTER 20
WHAT TO EXPECT NEXT

I had written two-thirds of this book when the final report from the Royal Commission into Aged Care Quality and Safety was released on 1 March 2021. Like many colleagues, providers, representatives from peak bodies and consumers, I spent the following weekend pouring over the 326 pages of the report and digesting what the 148 recommendations would mean for the industry, but more specifically, for the people at the centre of this Commission's purpose: our older loved ones.

These 148 recommendations are going to create a fundamental shift in the way the aged-care system operates moving forward. The current research and subsequent proposed changes and implementation of the recommendations are shaking up the industry across many domains such as funding, governance, workforce and the demonstrated delivery of quality and meaningful care to our older loved ones. There are big changes coming, and we're scrambling to anticipate what these changes will mean across many aspects of in-home and residential care.

For the people who are waiting to access the aged-care system, to receive the support they need and to understand that they have a voice in the direction of their care, we're wondering if the imminent changes are going to be enabling or, by haste in design and implementation, disabling. Will the changes that are coming empower our older loved ones? Or further disempower them?

Will the changes give our older loved ones greater self-determination to direct the kind of services or support they want to receive at home, or will they be constrained by a new model that will 'classify' people's needs based on their use of service events only?

I've stepped you through what the aged-care system looks like now, providing you with an insider's view to preparing for and sourcing the kind of care that is most appropriate for your older loved one. With this information you'll be well placed to access the services and support your older loved one's needs to remain living at home.

And now I'm going to rattle that position with an explanation of what I'm seeing emerging with the reforms. But don't worry, the knowledge and understanding you've gained from the previous sections in this book will equip you to approach the coming changes with clarity and confidence.

THE PRINCIPLES OF AGED CARE DON'T CHANGE

The principles of empowered ageing, of you being enabled to drive a conversation and to advocate for your older loved one don't change because a system is overhauled and programs and processes change.

I won't be commenting on all 148 recommendations but highlighting those that will have a direct impact on assessment, approvals and access to in-home care. In the following chapters, you will be presented with an explanation of these recommendations from the Final Report of the Royal Commission into Aged Care Quality and Safety and how they are likely to impact you, the people seeking to support your older loved ones at home:

- Recommendation 25: A new aged care program
- Recommendation 28: A single comprehensive assessment process
- Recommendation 29: Care finders to support navigation of aged care
- Recommendation 31: Approved provider's responsibility for care management.

There is an abundance of consultation and review occurring at the time of writing this book as various organisations have been tasked by the Australian Government Department of Health to develop new models that reflect the Commission's recommendations.

The Department has published a consultation calendar that steps through proposed dates for the workshops, focus groups and bilateral discussions during 2022.[1] This consultation involves webinars and surveys where these organisations are inviting the input of consumers, providers, peak bodies, health professionals and academics to shape the formation of a new aged-care program and a new assessment workforce and process, to establish the Care Finder and Care Manager roles, and to transition the current system to the new one. It's anticipated these consultations will have concluded in June 2022.

---

1 www.health.gov.au/sites/default/files/documents/2022/03/support-at-home-consultation-calendar_2.pdf.

From July 2023, it is proposed that the recommendations will be introduced. At the time of writing this book, the government is already moving to transition the sector to this new design.

In the following chapters, I'll discuss what we know now about in-home care provision and what is anticipated to change, and reaffirm your position as central to facilitating thorough assessments, advocating for appropriate approvals and access to personalised support, and ensuring you know what to do when your older loved one's needs change over time.

CHAPTER 21
A NEW AGED-CARE PROGRAM

Commissioner Briggs, in discussing the need for a new aged-care program, cites the complexity and fragmentation in the way aged care has been organised to date. The existing range of programs overlap as well as leaving gaps in service provision.[1]

Further, programs are not easy to use or even understand, and the aim of a new aged-care program should be to provide care and support to older people to preserve and restore their independence and their capacity for dignified living: 'Older people should be supported to remain in their own homes for as long as possible, because this is where they want to be. The new program design will put much greater emphasis on care at home.'[2]

Recommendation 25 in the Final Report describes the new aged-care program as combining the three existing programs that we are familiar with, being the Commonwealth Home Support Programme,

---

1   The Final Report for the Royal Commission into Aged Care Quality and Safety, *Care, Dignity and Respect*, pages 35–37.

2   The Final Report for the Royal Commission into Aged Care Quality and Safety, *Care, Dignity and Respect*, page 37.

the Home Care Packages Program and Short-Term Restorative Care. The key points concerning this recommendation are:

'a. a common set of eligibility criteria identifying a need (whether of a social, psychological or physical character) to prevent or delay deterioration in a person's capacity to function independently, or to ameliorate the effects of such deterioration, and to enhance the person's ability to live independently as well as possible, for as long as possible

b. an entitlement to all forms of support and care which the individual is assessed as needing

c. a single assessment process based upon a common assessment framework and arrangements followed by all assessors

d. certainty of funding and availability based on assessment need

e. genuine choice and flexibility accorded to each individual about how their aged care needs are to be met (including choice of provider and level of engagement in managing care, and appropriate and adapted supports to enable people from diverse backgrounds and experiences to exercise choice)

f. access to one or multiple categories of the aged care program simultaneously, based on need

g. portability of entitlement between providers throughout Australia.'

The proposed merging of the Commonwealth Home Support Programme, the Home Care Package Program and Short-Term Restorative Care into one will be known as the Support at Home Program, and an overview of this new program discusses how this is being designed: 'Improved supports in the home would prevent senior Australians from having to enter residential aged care prematurely and against their wishes. If done well, it may mean people don't need to enter residential aged care at all.'[3]

I don't disagree. We know older people want to remain living in their homes for as long as possible, but a serious injection of funding, recruitment and retention of carer workforce and timely access to the right support to allow someone to stay in their own home is needed. A new aged-care program also needs to address choice and flexibility and allow the recipient of the funding to determine what services and support are meaningful to them as their health needs change.

Also, if a new aged-care program can genuinely enable older people to remain living in their own homes for as long as possible, a seismic cultural shift in the way we view the possibility of this option also needs to occur. The cultural shift needs to occur in hospitals, in GP practices and across the wider community. Convincing hospital clinicians, GPs and the adult children of older people that an improved aged-care program is a viable alternative to entry into a residential aged-care facility is going to be met with a healthy dose of scepticism.

THE SUPPORT AT HOME PROGRAM

Let's take a broad look at this new program, the Support at Home Program, which is expected to be introduced in July 2023.

The Support at Home Program Overview recognises that in-home aged care currently consists of several programs that have different approaches to assessment, eligibility, service provision,

---

3   Support at Home Program overview paper, January 2022, page 4. www.health.gov.au/ sites/default/files/documents/2022/01/support-at-home-program-overview.pdf.

funding and fees. This overview states that this current system can lead to inequitable outcomes for older people as people with the same needs receive different supports. The overview also recognises that the current system entails long wait times for services and support and some service availability is variable depending on location.

The new Support at Home Program is seeking to streamline the assessment process, determine access to a range of services based on need rather than allocating a 'level' of package, and create flexibility for older people in how they choose to spend their funding.

The Support at Home Program also proposes a new program for goods, equipment, assistive technologies (GEAT) and home modifications. Under current arrangements, recipients of CHSP can possibly access up to $1000 for GEAT and up to $10,000 for home modifications. Actual availability of this is limited due to the low amount of this type of funding available.

With funding under the Home Care Package program, people are required to 'save up' for these types of items or services, meaning they'll need to forgo other aspects of their care to accrue funding to spend on technology or bathroom modifications, for example.

In all my years in the sector, I haven't known anyone who has been successful in receiving this type of funding for these types of services under CHSP, and I've known many who are receiving Home Care Packages who have had to 'save up' for items such as a personal alarm or bathroom modification because their package funding had reached its limit, including my own mum.

A maxed out package

My mum was the recipient of a Home Care Package level 2. She had her package managed by a fully managed or traditional package provider, meaning the provider arranged all of Mum's services and support.

Mum's package funding was maxed out on domestic assistance, lawn mowing, occasional washing of her dog and occasional cleaning of her car. These last two services were offered as both posed a fall risk to my mum, who is unable to bend down or reach to complete these tasks. She also received a personal alarm that incurred a monthly monitoring fee, and the fee was deducted from her package funding.

My sister and I contributed by cooking meals, also washing her dog when we were able, attending to larger cleaning tasks within her home such as cleaning the fans and air conditioners, and performing extended yard maintenance such as pruning to keep the garden free from hazardous overgrowth. My husband and son completed home maintenance tasks for my mum.

Mum had a fall in the park. She didn't have her mobile phone with her and she was unable to notify anyone she was in trouble. The personal alarm that she had was only for use within her home, and it wasn't a falls-detecting alarm, so she hadn't taken it to the park. She lay on the ground until she eventually managed to stand up again. She was bruised, but thankfully didn't sustain any broken bones.

It was distressing for her and for us. I did some research and found a fabulous new personal alarm that had a falls detection feature and GPS tracking, so the alarm could be tracked to any location where Mum might have needed help.

It was an obvious decision to purchase this new alarm that could pinpoint her whereabouts and then send out a text message and a phone call to all of the six contacts included in the device, including 000.

I knew Mum's package funding was maxed out and we couldn't reduce any of her current services to redirect funds. The cost of this new alarm? Just over $500. I had to buy the new alarm myself. I also bought Mum a high-back chair with arm rests, as she couldn't get out of the lower chair anymore. This chair also cost just over $500.

Spending $1000 to ensure my mum's safety in and around home was never an issue for me. What was an issue was having no alternative when her funding was at the limit and there was no access to any other type of funding to procure these two items.

CARE MANAGEMENT

Another issue that is generating some interesting discussion within the stakeholder groups I've been participating in recently is the development of a new service: 'Care Management'.

Care Management is recognised as adding consistent and experienced support to older people with more complex needs. The aim of Care Management is to provide oversight and assist with coordination of in-home care.

The discussions surrounding the development of this role or service at present include:

- Who is the most appropriate workforce to fulfil this role?
    - those with vocational training
    - tertiary qualified and experienced clinicians?

- Who is the most appropriate recipient for eligibility for Care Management?
- Is someone excluded from being approved to access Care Management if they have a designated carer?
- How is the independence of Care Managers to ensure accountability with advocacy with Home Care Package providers to be managed?

* * *

The latter part of 2022 and early 2023 as we move towards the implementation of the reforms in July 2023 will reveal the outcomes of the many consultation processes and trials that will eventually define this new Support at Home Program.

In the following chapters, I'll take a closer look at the specific aspects of the recommendations from the Final Report with regards to assessment and how older people may or may not be better able to access the support they need to remain living at home under the new aged-care program.

CHAPTER 22

A SINGLE COMPREHENSIVE ASSESSMENT PROCESS

THE CHALLENGES OF THE CURRENT SYSTEM

Older people seeking in-home services and support are presently assessed by one or both assessment services, being the RAS and ACAT, as discussed in previous chapters. These assessments follow from the screening process when registering someone with My Aged Care.

By the time an older person is assessed by the ACAT, they are often confused about why they have been previously assessed and the need to be assessed again. Older people and their families tell me they have been 'assessed by My Aged Care'. This statement isn't entirely correct; it is not an assessment that My Aged Care completes, it's a screening process to determine which might be the most appropriate assessment service to direct that person to.

Older people and their families also tell me that the RAS assessors are My Aged Care assessors, and they tell me the ACAT is the My Aged Care assessor. Again, this is not completely accurate;

a RAS or an ACAT assessor is separate to the My Aged Care screening process.

Multiple levels of enquiry can result in an older person having been 'assessed' five times before they actually receive some types of services.

It is not difficult to see why older people and their families are confused by the process.

These multiple layers of enquiry or assessment generate confusion in older people and their family carers and cause some people to stop moving forward in the system because they believe they have already been 'assessed'. They don't realise it is an evolving and ongoing process of review to determine access to more support as frailty increases and health declines.

The Department of Health has recognised the challenges these multiple levels of screening and assessment pose to people who are trying to understand and navigate the system, and discussion surrounding streamlining the assessment process has been occurring in recent years. In 2017, the Legislated Review of Aged Care reviewed nine aspects of the 2011 Productivity Commission report *Caring for Older Australians* and the subsequent Living Longer, Living Better reforms that arose from that report. Their report recommended 38 improvements, with recommendation 27 being that 'the government integrate the RAS and ACAT assessment workforces'.[1]

---

1   www.health.gov.au/resources/publications/legislated-review-of-aged-care-2017-report, page 6.

A NEW ASSESSMENT PROCESS

After much investigation, in the Royal Commission's Final Report in February 2021 a single assessment process was recommended and, after a trial process, aims to be implemented by July 2023.

This new assessment process will replace the two assessment services we are currently familiar with, being the Regional Assessment Service (RAS) and the Aged Care Assessment Team (ACAT).

The dissolution of the RAS and, more concerning, the ACAT to be merged into a new yet-to-be-named assessment workforce, have generated a strong response within the community over the past couple of years and are provoking impassioned discussion at present about what this new workforce will look like. Under a new assessment framework, it's not that the ACATs will be privatised as had been raised as a possibility. Instead, it is anticipated the ACATs will no longer have a role. The ACATs will cease to exist.

Recommendation 28 from the Final Report details the new assessment process should:

'a. be undertaken by an assessor who is independent from approved providers, so that a person's level of funding should be determined independently of the approved provider

b. occur, wherever possible, before funded services commence, although funded services may be offered on an interim basis pending assessment where this is necessary in the opinion of a care finder

c. be efficient and scalable according to the complexity of needs and vulnerability of the older person

d. be forward-looking and promote older people's autonomy and self-determination

e. include assessment of the need for care management and the intensity and complexity of that need

f. include an assessment of any informal carer's needs

g. use multidisciplinary teams for more complex needs'.

The design of this new model is provided in the Support at Home Program Overview (January 2022).

A new assessment workforce will utilise a new assessment tool. The Integrated Assessment Tool (IAT) will replace the National Screening and Assessment Form that is currently used by both RAS and ACAT assessors.

This new tool is proposed to comprise four levels of assessment and 'each level of assessment will build on the previous, using trigger points to guide assessors to the most appropriate assessment level for each person'.[2] In addition, the Integrated Assessment Tool 'would also identify the home care services that are most appropriate to meet their aged care needs using a new classification system' and 'the assessment process will identify if a senior Australian's needs would be best met in residential aged care'.

Given that it is possible we may lose the expertise of the ACATs and potentially move towards a non-clinician workforce using an assessment tool that identifies services that are most appropriate to meet the older person's needs, I can't help but wonder if we are moving further away from consumer-directed care.

It is also unnerving to note that the IAT will identify if a senior Australian's needs would be best met in residential aged care. What if the older person doesn't want to enter residential aged care and wants to remain at home? Will the IAT and this new workforce have the scope and ability to consider what the person wants?

---

2   Support at Home Program Overview, page 5.

A bumpy ride

I was contacted by a couple, seeking information for the wife. She had been assessed by the RAS two years previously and although she had been approved for some referral codes, she had not received any CHSP services.

The husband was confused about how the system worked and wanted to know how to access services and support for his wife. This couple are both in their 90s and are both well-educated.

The wife has a complex health history and has become increasingly frail and dependent on her husband over the past two years. I completed a comprehensive assessment and wrote a detailed report demonstrating the older lady's unmet needs, goals that aligned with a program of restorative care and need for coordinated support in the future. I was very clear that the couple were struggling and if something happened to the husband, the wife would be unable to remain at home without formal support.

This lady would benefit from receiving a Short-Term Restorative Care (STRC) package and then a Home Care Package. This lady needed an ACAT assessment.

As this lady had previously been assessed by the RAS, the referral I made via My Aged Care for a support plan review would go firstly to the RAS for review before being forwarded to the ACAT.

Sometimes the RAS assessor will call me to discuss my referral before forwarding to the ACAT, sometimes they won't. Either way, as long as the referral follows the path it should and reaches the ACAT, it's fine by me.

The husband had informed me after some weeks that they were going to be assessed. A RAS assessor came to their home. My client advised me the RAS assessor spent half the time they were there telling them about his role within the organisation. My client also reported that he felt the RAS assessor made 'light' of their situation.

The RAS assessor did not contact me and did not refer on to the ACAT.

I was concerned about the feedback from my client. I contacted the company who is responsible for the RAS workforce in that state. I spoke with the RAS assessor. We discussed my client's presentation. The RAS assessor was unaware of STRC. He agreed with my assessment about this client's functional decline but was reluctant to refer onto the ACAT.

I pressed my case, and we had a 30-minute conversation whereby I gave him a rapid introduction to STRC and the proposed reforms, particularly the Support at Home Program. Enabled with the right information and an understanding of why this lady needed STRC, the RAS assessor forwarded my referral to the ACAT.

24 hours later, the ACAT had made contact with my client and was scheduling an assessment.

The RAS assessor had no idea about these coming reforms, or what the changes might entail for his workforce or the clients he may see in another 12 months.

I'm not saying that the RAS workforce is going to become the new assessment workforce under the Support at Home Program, but it is possible. The risk with this workforce being neither clinically orientated nor knowledgeable and experienced in the domains of older person's care may leave an already vulnerable cohort of older people further disadvantaged. Comprehensive assessment is the expertise of a workforce such as the ACAT.

* * *

A single assessment will assist in reducing the need for people to tell their story over and over again. A comprehensive assessment will position the older person to get it right the first time, the assessor teasing out the implications of health conditions, emerging or diagnosed cognitive impairment and mood disorders, and being able to predict the trajectory of further functional decline, social isolation and impending reliance on carers to meet their needs after they have been assessed.

Can a single assessment also be a comprehensive assessment? It can, but only with the retention of a specialised workforce that includes the experience of assessors such as ACAT clinicians.

CHAPTER 23

CARE FINDERS TO SUPPORT NAVIGATION OF THE AGED-CARE SYSTEM

Australia's aged-care system is convoluted. My Aged Care, the gateway and initial touchpoint to access government-subsidised services and support, is a maze. Assessments, approvals and understanding how to engage providers to deliver the support needed at home is defeating in its complexity.

How do you find the right information to know how to make decisions that are right for your older loved one? And how do you know the information you're receiving is independent and trustworthy? Where do you go to source support in your local area, support that aligns with your loved one's preferences?

CARE FINDERS

The Final Report of the Royal Commission recommended 'Care Finders' to support navigation of the aged-care system. Recommendation 29 highlights the following points:

'1. From July 2023, the Australian Government should fund the engagement of a workforce of personal advisors to older people, their families and carers, called "care finders".

2. The function of care finders will be to assist older people seeking aged care services with information about the aged care system and case management services by:

   a. providing face-to-face support to older people to help them identify the best options for care to meet their individual needs and goals, to exercise informed choice, and to understand their entitlements. That support should be scalable and proportionate to need and vulnerability

   b. assisting older people to understand, gain access to and participate in assessments and reassessments of needs and eligibility for aged care, and work closely with the local assessment team to facilitate the assessment process

   c. ascertaining the best options for services in the local area and link them to these options. This might involve linking the older person to services outside the aged care system, such as housing, mental health or health care more generally

   d. following up to make sure that referrals have been accepted and the support and care identified in the assessment is in place

e. conducting regular check-ins with the older person to ensure that the services are meeting their needs

f. where changes in needs occur, or services are not meeting needs, taking the necessary steps in consultation with the older person, including reassessment or referrals to services.'

Care Finders to support and advocate for older people within the aged-care system have historically only been associated with residential aged-care facilities and have also been known as 'placement consultants'. A Google search for 'care finders' elicits results that are predominantly orientated to helping people choose a residential aged-care home.

Some of these organisations are independent and some work as brokers for the companies that own the aged-care facilities, taking a commission for successful placements in any given facility.

It is reassuring to see that the government is providing funding to an organisation that is not aligned with Home Care Package providers to establish and maintain this network of Care Finders as public concern about maintaining independence from Home Care Package providers has been a topic of interest in the community. As we move towards the implementation of the reforms in mid 2023, the Federal Government has committed to ongoing funding and the development of a Services Australia–based model of support for older people needing advice regarding aged care.

The 2021–22 Budget details:

- 'a new government face-to-face aged care service will be available in up to 325 Services Australia service centres in all states and territories, to provide information on aged care services and assist people to use online channels

- new face-to-face aged care specialists will be available in 70 Services Australia service centres in all states and territories, and include mobile service centres to reach rural and regional areas. These specialists will connect consumers with local services, financial information services, social workers, interpreters and advocates.'[1]

SO WHAT DOES A CARE FINDER DO?

An Aged Care Navigator or Care Finder has a deep understanding of how Australia's aged-care system works. An Aged Care Navigator or Care Finder also has a broad knowledge of the programs and services that exist outside the aged-care system that people can access to enhance the support they receive from Commonwealth-subsidised aged-care services.

An Aged Care Navigator or Care Finder will support an older person or their family carer to understand how My Aged Care works and prepare them for the initial contact or registration with this gateway. They will explain how a RAS or ACAT assessment is conducted and ensure older people are able to articulate their needs in detail, so they'll get the right approvals for a range of services and support.

An Aged Care Navigator or Care Finder will liaise with and advocate for an older person with their GP, hospital clinicians, social support organisations and service providers. They'll go into bat for the older person if they feel the older person's voice isn't being heard or their wishes are being dismissed. Essentially, an

---

1   www.health.gov.au/sites/default/files/documents/2021/05/home-care-pillar-1-of-the-royal-commission-response-connecting-senior-australians-to-aged-care-services.pdf.

Aged Care Navigator or Care Finder is the older person's ally within the aged-care system.

AGED CARE SPECIALIST OFFICERS

My team and I are always trawling the internet ensuring we keep ourselves up to date and aware of any announcements relating to the aged-care system. We aim to keep our fingers on the pulse of changes within our industry so we can share this information with our clients and followers and the wider community.

Recently we came across the service Aged Care Specialist Officer (ACSO) on the website of Services Australia. The role of ACSO as detailed on the Services Australia webpage notes that the ACSO can help with:

- 'providing in-depth information on the different types of aged care services
- checking if you're eligible for government-funded services and making a referral for an aged care assessment
- helping you appoint a representative for My Aged Care
- providing financial information about aged care services
- connecting you to local support services'.[2]

The webpage also states, 'You can book a free face-to-face appointment with an ACSO in some locations across Australia'.

We were really excited to stumble across this information and keen to share it widely. We thought this might be the introduction of the Care Finders who were based in Services Australia local

---

2   www.servicesaustralia.gov.au/aged-care-specialist-officer-my-aged-care-face-to-face-services?context=55715.

offices. So we called the number listed on the Services Australia website. We called a few times. Sometimes we got through after an extended wait, sometimes an automated message advised 'all our service operators are busy at this time, please call back later'.

When we were able to connect to someone, the person on the end of the phone did not know about this service. We explained what we were reading on the web page and were told that this service is only for financial advice for people with complex financial issues who are looking to move into residential placement.

We explained again that the web page listed several services that related to the aged-care system, including providing in-depth information on the different types of aged-care services, checking for eligibility and making a referral to My Aged Care.

We were told that the service is only available if the person is already registered with My Aged Care.

We got nowhere.

We checked out the My Aged Care website and learned that the ACSO service launched in November 2021, servicing 16 locations, with plans to roll out to another 80 locations by December 2022.

It's possible that 'Aged Care Specialist Officer' is the term Services Australia is going to use for the centre-based Care Finders. It may not be. We'll keep watching this space and trying to get to the bottom of this, but any information we share will be after you're reading this book and will be via our blogs and social media.

* * *

Recommendation 29 in the Final Report highlighted a gap within the industry and stipulated how this much-needed and valuable role would assist older people and their families to navigate the aged-care system.

Trials have been underway for the past four years and funding has been announced to embed Care Finders into local communities via an independent organisation. As we move towards July 2023, older people and their families and carers should remain optimistic that there will be a workforce dedicated to providing the support they need to navigate the maze that is Australia's aged-care system.

CHAPTER 24

WHAT ARE A PROVIDER'S CARE RESPONSIBILITIES?

Under the current model of in-home care provision, a Home Care Package provider administers the package funding on behalf of the person assigned the package. We've discussed the two main models, being fully managed, and self-managed. Within these models, the provider takes fees for the management of the government funding, and these fees are usually described as being any combination of 'administration fees', 'care coordination fees' or 'care management fees'.

So, given a package provider is charging fees to deliver and coordinate these services and support, you would think they would be monitoring your loved one's situation, acting in a timely manner in response to their failing health and increasing frailty and need for more support, and referring back to My Aged Care for a support plan review if they need a package upgrade ... right?

You'd also think your package provider would be telling you about options for other services or support outside the aged-care system; for example, applying for the carer's allowance, a disability parking permit, payments under other national- and state-funded programs and the supplements attached to Home Care Packages, such as the dementia and cognition supplement.

Well, some package providers do this, and they do it well, and other providers do not.

A missed opportunity

I was in the office of a local Home Care Package provider. The senior care worker was speaking with a lady about overnight respite for her mother. The care worker asked me a question about medication, and me being the kind of person I am, I started talking to this lady about her mother, who was coming to stay at the respite centre for a few days.

The provider who runs this day and overnight respite centre specialises in dementia care.

The lady mentioned she had recently moved her mother from a different fully managed provider to self-management and she was managing the Home Care Package on behalf of her mother. I asked this lady if her mother was receiving the dementia and cognition supplement, to which she replied, 'Oh no, Mum doesn't have dementia'.

I replied that a person doesn't need to have a diagnosis of dementia to be eligible for this supplement, which would give the older lady additional funding on top of her package funding.

I was curious now and asked the lady why her older mother was staying at a respite centre that specialised in dementia care. She recounted the story of how her mother had had a stroke eight years previously and was now unable to manage her day-to-day decisions and activities.

I said to this lady, 'Let me ask you one question, and if you answer yes to this question, I'll take 10 minutes to complete the screening tool that demonstrates eligibility for the supplement, and we'll see if we can get your mum a bit of extra funding.'

I asked this lady the question and she answered 'yes'. The question was, 'Does she have difficulty finding her way around familiar places when alone, like the local shops?' This question is the first question on one of the screening tools used to check eligibility for the dementia and cognition supplement, the Psychogeriatric Assessment Scale (informant). I then proceeded to complete the eligibility tool with the daughter, and it was abundantly clear the older lady was eligible for the supplement. But here's the kicker: this older lady's fully managed package provider had been managing her care for eight years. That's potentially eight years that the older lady could have been receiving this additional funding.

This provider is a well-known and dominant industry provider.

I completed the application form for the supplement right then and there and gave it to this lady to give to her self-managed provider, and encouraged her to follow up and ensure the supplement was allocated to her mum's package funding.

Why the package provider hadn't screened for eligibility for this supplement is anyone's guess. It may have been because they didn't have a registered nurse on staff who could complete the screening. Maybe they did have a registered nurse but their workload was so great they weren't able to review this lady. Whatever the reason, missing such a simple aspect of this person's care provision over possibly eight years which would have enabled additional funding that would provide more support is not acceptable.

Recommendation 31 of the Final Report details approved providers' responsibilities for care management:

'1. From 1 July 2022, a person's approved provider must assign a care manager to the person unless an assessment team has assessed the person as eligible for home care and, in future, "care at home" without the need for any care management.

2. In the case of home care and, in future, "care at home", if the person has more than one approved provider, the person's lead provider must assign a care manager to the person.

3. Care management should be scaled to match the complexity of the older person's needs and should be provided in a manner that respects any wishes of the person to be involved in the management of their care.

4. The care manager should:

    a. have relevant qualifications and experience suitable for the range and complexity of the care needs of the people to whom the care manager provides care management

    b. consult with the person and, if applicable, their carer, to develop a comprehensive support and care plan, including activities to promote various aspects of health and wellbeing and to enhance their ability to live or participate in the community and address their strengths, capability, aspirations, and goals

c. implement, monitor and review the support and care plan, and adjust as appropriate

d. meet the requirements for care management set out in the person's care plan and (if applicable) personalised budget for home care and, in future, "care at home".

One would ask, if Home Care Package providers are taking fees for care coordinating or care managing, why have so many older people not received the support they need? Why has it taken a Royal Commission to identify and recommend how coordinated care within Home Care Packages should be?

Because care coordination or management is the exception and not the norm across the industry. Too many providers sign people up to deliver their Home Care Package and then they're not reviewed again. I know this is a bold statement, but I've seen this situation so often, and it happened to my mum too.

A NEW WORKFORCE OF CARE MANAGERS?

So, what can we hope will be a good model for a new workforce of Care Managers?

The Support at Home Program Overview (January 2022) notes care management being a service type within this new model: 'Care management would be offered to senior Australians who have a more complex mix of services and need oversight and coordination of their care. Funding for care management would be restricted, so that people are not able to swap their care management for any other service.'

What this statement means is that under the new Support at Home Program, people will be approved to receive funding for Care Management if the assessor believes they need a Care Manager. Not everyone will be approved for the Care Management service. It also means that if someone is approved to receive funding for a Care Manager, that service cannot be interchanged with domestic assistance or lawn mowing or personal care; the funding is to be used solely for Care Management.

At the time of writing, there is an abundance of research and stakeholder engagement for the development of the Support at Home Program. Care management within this model is being discussed, and stakeholders that are being asked to offer thoughts on a care management workforce have debated non-clinical versus clinical Care Managers.

Eligibility to be allocated funding to access a Care Manager has also been discussed. The conversation has considered who needs a Care Manager; only people with complex health needs or all people receiving in-home care?

Those who are self-managing their Home Care Package have also been identified as people who should be eligible for Care Management. I've also heard arguments for people who have carers supporting the self-management of an older loved one's Home Care Package fulfilling the role of Care Manager informally, therefore making the recipient of the Home Care Package ineligible to access a Care Manager.

From my experience, I think everyone should be eligible for Care Management. And I am an advocate for registered nurses fulfilling the role of Care Manager. Registered nurses bring a holistic approach, understand health conditions and medications, and can reasonably predict the trajectory of complex and chronic health conditions that will impact on a person's wellbeing and independence. Understanding a person's health conditions, knowing what that means in the context of threatened independence and being able to liaise with the older person's GP, package provider and allied health clinical support team are essential to ensuring comprehensive care planning and management.

* * *

The discussion regarding the design of the Support at Home Program is giving us a real opportunity to develop a much-needed role to support recipients of in-home care to get the support they need within ideal timeframes.

Though it is reasonable to expect that people receiving in-home care from Home Care Package provision should be engaged, reviewed and monitored to ensure their needs are being identified and acted upon, in reality this is far from what happens in many instances at present.

With the introduction of Care Managers, Home Care Package providers will need to take a proactive approach and will be expected to be more accountable for managing and coordinating the support a person receives from their package funding. The implementation of Care Managers could really make a difference to older people living at home by enabling participative discussion and planning to support them to remain where they want to be: at home.

CONCLUSION

Australia's aged-care system is complex and confusing.

People liken it to a minefield. And that description is fitting.

It's not surprising people often ask, *what the heck do I do?*

Being lost in the aged-care system can delay access to the right level of in-home support for up to 18 months. Not understanding the difference between the assessment teams or the approval outcomes or how the national priority queue works all add up to delaying access to the support your older loved one needs to remain at home.

I've written this book as an insider's take on the information you won't find on the My Aged Care website, what you won't be told by a RAS or ACAT assessor, and what to do after your older loved one has had their assessment and is wondering 'what happens next?'

I encourage you to put into action what you've learned reading this book.

I've also introduced you to the biggest change the industry is confronting now: the implementation of major reforms. The Support at Home Program will look completely different to the CHSP, HCP and STRC programs that are available now. These three programs will be merged onto one.

There is an abundance of research, consultation and stakeholder engagement occurring as we speak. Some in the industry believe the change is too great and happening too quickly to be introduced in July 2023. Others disagree and are preparing themselves for this new model. With the recent change of government, we're also wondering if this will delay the introduction of the reforms or allow for review of certain aspects of the proposed changes.

Whatever happens in July next year, what you've learned in this book will allow you to be prepared for the coming changes.

Take some time now to reflect on what you've learned in this book. Take some more time to consider your older loved one's needs and how much support you're offering them to remain in their home.

The next step is to start compiling a list of everything you do for them, and everything their friends and neighbours do for them.

We have a checklist that you're welcome to download and use to get you started.

We also offer a no-obligation, free phone call to discuss your queries and we're happy to tell you if you're on the right path or maybe need some guidance.

We're passionate about empowering people like you with knowledge and 'know how', to get the right outcomes for your older loved one.

It *is* possible to access the support and services your older loved one needs to remain at home, in a timely manner, just as I did for my dad and am doing now for my mum.

You're one step closer now to being able to facilitate that, because you now know what the heck you need to do.

My story

I'm the eldest of four kids, I have two sisters and a brother. My mum had the four of us within five years. We grew up in far north Queensland. I had what I think was a typical childhood, growing up in the '70s and '80s.

My parents were both teachers. We went to the local Catholic and state public schools, played sport, learned the piano, rode our bikes with our friends until the lights came on in the evening and we scurried home in time for dinner. Dinner around the table was when we all reconnected and shared our stories of the day.

We used to holiday in Cooktown. My dad loved Cooktown. When my dad's mum had a stroke, our holidays became a long drive south to Brisbane to visit nanna in hospital and then in the nursing home.

Those were long drives, with the four of us crammed into the back of the car. And passing the days at the hospital and then at the nursing home wasn't so much fun for us kids. But this was what we did as a family. We came together and supported each other when we needed to.

I was young, but I knew that this was what you did when your loved ones needed you. You rolled your sleeves up and did what needed to be done to take care of each other.

I became a nurse. I trained at my local hospital, then went on and completed my tertiary studies. I cared about people, and I loved my job.

I'd worked in all sorts of exciting and fulfilling clinical roles and in management, but it wasn't until I joined the ACAT that I realised I'd found my niche. I stayed with the ACAT for nine years, then moved into a very specialised role, a nurse navigator, where I was able to define my own model and fill the gaps in what I believed was missing within the public hospital system and community aged care.

During this time, my dad was becoming absent-minded, and his mood was low. I encouraged him to speak to his GP about a geriatrician review, which he did and he was diagnosed with depression.

Over the next two years, Dad's memory continued to fail him, gradually, and he was then diagnosed with Mild Cognitive Impairment (MCI). I knew Dad would go on to develop dementia. And he did.

It was no surprise to me.

Over the course of 18 months, he declined cognitively and functionally. During this time, in his last 12 months he also had four strokes, each time being admitted to hospital.

Amazingly Dad bounced back from the first three strokes but the fourth one left him with significant functional deficits, at least for the first couple of months. Each time he was admitted to hospital he developed delirium. This was incredibly difficult.

My mum and my younger sister and I took turns to stay with Dad in hospital. I took the 'night shifts'.

Dad was so lost and vulnerable in those deliriums. It still rattles me when I remember how desperately terrified he was during the hallucinations the delirium brought on.

I had taken leave from my job to support my mum and dad during these difficult times.

My son, who was in his early 20s, used to visit his granddad after work and on weekends to give us a break. My daughter, though at university, would have come home if we'd asked her.

And when my husband – a FIFO worker – was home, he kept the dogs fed and the house running while I slept during the day.

During this fourth hospital admission, his last hospital admission, I gave a lot of thought about where Dad was going to be discharged to. We wanted to take him home. I'd discussed it with Mum and my younger sister; we'd let our other sister who lives in Perth know and we told our brother who lives in Sydney.

When I raised this with Dad's treating team, they were sceptical. Dad was still a two-person transfer, though close to only needing one person to transfer. Dad's treating team referred him to the TCP team, who accepted him onto the program and facilitated his transition back home.

It was hard. I wondered if we could really manage this. My sister flew over from Perth to support us during this time.

But over the 12 weeks Dad was on TCP he improved. He regained his strength and was able to get himself out of a chair and walk, supervised, around the house. After TCP finished, Dad's HCP 4 recommenced.

By this time, we were exhausted. My mum was a rock. We looked to her to give us strength, and she did.

We had carers coming every day, even on weekends initially until his accumulated HCP funding ran out. I began showering Dad after work and on weekends. My brother came up from Sydney to give us a break and my daughter flew home when she could from Brisbane.

It was a team effort.

Dad's dementia progressed and eventually his function declined again, and I knew we were moving towards his end of life.

There wasn't enough funding in Dad's HCP for ongoing weekly support, so we were paying for carers as well and we hired an electric hospital-type bed with a pressure-relieving mattress. Dad came home after that fourth stoke in August 2017. By December I knew we only had weeks left with Dad.

We decided that whatever happened we wouldn't be calling the ambulance again. Dad was not going to go to hospital because we knew he would die there, and keeping him at home, to die surrounded by his family, was our commitment to Dad and each other.

But I was afraid. I didn't let on to my mum or my siblings, but there was one thing I knew we couldn't manage at home and if that happened, we'd have to call an ambulance and have Dad taken to hospital. And I knew he'd never survive that, which we'd accepted, but dying in hospital was something we couldn't accept.

I was afraid Dad would have a fall and break his hip.

I couldn't manage that kind of pain at home. I actually prayed every day that Dad wouldn't fall. And I cried. A lot.

We had our last Christmas with him in 2017.

Dad was so frail by this time. He was barely eating, he couldn't verbalise, though he tried. He was still walking but we also pushed him around the house in a wheelchair when he was too weak.

He never fell.

My brother came up from Sydney to be with Dad one last time.

My GP and dad's geriatrician were on speed dial, and I'd call them to ask their advice and to request scripts for when Dad became agitated, distressed or when in the last couple of days he developed pain.

Dad's carer Kath was our source of support.

You know the saying; it takes a village? Well, it did.

Dad knew he could leave us, but he just kept hanging in there. My sister was on her way over from Perth. When my sister arrived and went into the bedroom, Dad opened his eyes and held her hand. He knew who she was. He tried to say her name, but he couldn't.

There were a lot of tears.

We took photos and videos. We captured our dad's heart-breaking farewell.

At 9.47pm that night I took a photo of me holding hands with my dad. I said farewell to my dad.

I was driving home and something made me look at my watch at 10.22pm. My phone rang and it was my youngest sister who was at her own place, and she asked me if something had happened. We knew Dad had just left us.

We phoned our other sister who was with Dad, and she told us what we already knew.

I turned the car around.

My mum and my two sisters and I then sat there with Dad for the next couple of hours, drinking Kahlua, consoling each other, and recalling every special and funny moment that had happened over the past few weeks.

Dad was at last at peace and so were we because we'd managed to do what we had committed to each other to do, to keep Dad at home.

I'm a very private person and I've never written or spoken about my dad's death to anyone except my immediate family.

Why am I sharing my story so publicly?

Because it was just another aspect of our journey, my dad's journey. It's the path life takes us.

This book has been my purpose, and I know when I look back on my own life as I age, I'll know the words on these pages will have made a difference to the lives of so many older people and their families who are supporting them.

I've given you the knowledge and 'know how' to get better outcomes from our aged-care system. A system that often fails to support people with choice and dignity and self-determination as they age.

I've equipped you with the tools to enable confidence to discuss with My Aged Care, the RAS or ACAT assessors and providers of CHSP or Home Care Packages what person-centred care really is. It's not just words, it's your right.

I've shown you how to keep your older loved one at home for as long as you choose, knowing what services and support are available to you.

This story has been my path, my family's path.

My warmest regards to you as you now forge your own path, through the minefield that is our aged-care system. I know though, that you won't get lost now. You know exactly what the heck you need to do to support your loved ones as they age.

REFERENCES

Chapter 8

Commonwealth Home Support Programme (CHSP) Manual, www.health.gov.au/resources/publications/commonwealth-home-support-programme-chsp-manual

Commonwealth Home Support Programme Data Study, www.health.gov.au/resources/publications/commonwealth-home-support-programme-data-study

Fact Sheet: Commonwealth Home Support Programme (CHSP), www.gen-agedcaredata.gov.au/www_aihwgen/media/DoH-factsheets/CHSP-Fact-Sheet-2018-19.pdf?ext=.pdf

Home Care: Supporting senior Australians to remain independent for longer, www.health.gov.au/sites/default/files/documents/2022/04/budget-2022-23-home-care-supporting-senior-australians-to-remain-independent-for-longer.pdf

Chapter 9

NSAF User Guide: A guide to the information required to be considered and recorded during the My Aged Care assessment process, www.health.gov.au/sites/default/files/documents/2020/01/my-aged-care-national-screening-and-assessment-form-user-guide_0.pdf

Chapter 11

Council to investigate transition from aged and disability services, www.mildura.vic.gov.au/Latest-News/Council-to-investigate-transition-from-aged-and-disability-services

Moorabool Shire becomes latest local council to exit aged and disability care, www.theweeklysource.com.au/moorabool-shire-becomes-latest-local-council-to-exit-aged-and-disability-care/

Chapter 12

Aged Care Legislation Amendment (Increasing Consumer Choice) Bill 2016, www.aph.gov.au/Parliamentary_Business/Bills_Legislation/bd/bd1516a/16bd094#_ftnref53

Chapter 20

Support at Home Program Overview, Australian Government Department of Health, www.health.gov.au/sites/default/files/documents/2022/01/support-at-home-program-overview.pdf

Chapter 21

Support at Home Program Overview, Australian Government Department of Health, www.health.gov.au/sites/default/files/documents/2022/01/support-at-home-program-overview.pdf

Chapter 22

Legislated Review of Aged Care 2017 Report, www.health.gov.au/resources/publications/legislated-review-of-aged-care-2017-report

Options for the assessment, classification and funding model for the unified aged care at home program Final Report,

www.health.gov.au/sites/default/files/documents/2021/04/
options-for-an-assessment-classification-and-funding-model-for-
a-single-in-home-care-program.pdf

Support at Home Program Overview, Australian Government
Department of Health, www.health.gov.au/sites/default/files/
documents/2022/01/support-at-home-program-overview.pdf

Chapter 23

Royal Commission into Aged Care Quality and Safety Final
Report, agedcare.royalcommission.gov.au/publications/final-report

Chapter 24

Support at Home Program Overview, www.health.gov.au/sites/
default/files/documents/2022/01/support-at-home-program-
overview.pdf

ABOUT THE AUTHOR

Registered nurse, aged-care navigator and advocate Coral Wilkinson launched her award-winning business, See Me Aged Care Navigators, in 2019, responding to the confusion and distress people experience when trying to achieve timely access to in-home support for older loved ones.

As a former assessor and delegate with an Aged Care Assessment Team, Nurse Navigator and Clinical Nurse Consultant (older persons) within the public health system and having managed programs for both state and federally funded projects aimed at keeping older people well and in their own home, Coral's depth of professional experience enabled her to develop a model that addresses the challenges older people face in both the health and the aged-care sectors.

Working with providers of aged-care programs such as the Short-Term Restorative Care program and the Home Care Package program, Coral knows how good service provision is achievable in a community setting and supports people and providers to work together to optimise personalised care.

As a carer for her father, who had dementia and who remained at home through his end of life and presently supporting her mother, who still resides at home with the support of a Home Care Package level 4, Coral is committed to supporting others to achieve similar outcomes.

Coral is passionate about empowering people with knowledge and 'know how' to get the right approvals and timely support so their older loved ones can stay where they want to be, at home.

If you'd like to know more or discuss your loved one's situation with Coral and her team, you can reach to them via the website or connect with Coral and her team on their social networks.

Website

seemeacn.com.au

Socials

Facebook: facebook.com/seemeacn
LinkedIn: linkedin.com/in/coral-see-me-aged-care-navigators
Instagram: instagram.com/seemeagedcarenavigators